In Search of the Master Who Dances with Horses:
Growth

Andrew-Glyn Smail

Foreword

This book is the second part of a highly edited version of my posts on a blog written over the past few years until the time of publication, the first part being *In Search of the Master Who Dances with Horses: Challenge*. Like the latter book, it brings together the key posts in a format which offers all the conveniences which a traditional blog cannot.

First of all, the ebook format is portable, which means you can take this version of the blog with you and read it at your convenience wherever you are. Secondly, it is easier to read, because you do not have to be online to access it. Thirdly, it is searchable, making it easier to find and cross-reference information. Finally, it serves as a gateway to the blog itself, presenting the essence of the contents of the blog while offering access to it, should you wish to read an entire post and view its audio-visual content.

Klaus Ferdinand Hempfling

The blog was originally set up to catalogue my experiences and those of my partner as we prepared to spend a year living and studying full-time at Klaus Ferdinand Hempfling's Akedah International school in Denmark. It has turned out to be a record of a life-changing set of experiences, which is drawing a growing number of people from around the world to be part of its readership for no other reason I believe than that it represents a reasonable attempt on the part of a very ordinary person without any equestrian talents to become the kind of human a horse seeks to be with, a goal which I feel is the essence of what we should be trying to achieve with those sensitive creatures. I have decided to publish these posts in book form to make them available to those potential readers who have not yet discovered the blog.

For those of you who may not yet have heard of him, Klaus Ferdinand Hempfling is arguably the most popular horse trainer in the world based on social media statistics. At the time of writing just one of his numerous videos on YouTube had been viewed well over two million times (see http://www.youtube.com/watch?v= zq06bmJLt-U), while his official Facebook page had been liked by more than 675,000 people. By way of comparison Pat Parelli's official Facebook page had been liked by a little under 37,000 people, while that of Monty Roberts was still short of being liked by 307,000 people.

The secret to Hempfling's enormous popularity would appear to lie in his appeal to the growing number of horse owners and carers around the world who are looking for a new, meaningful way of being and interacting with horses.

Other horse people
Although some of the actions and teachings of Klaus Ferdinand Hempfling are dealt with extensively in both books, other great horse people have also left their impression on me in one form or another. Of these, Michael Bevilacqua, the main international representative of Nevzorov Haute Ecole, has been the most influential. Others include Linda Kohanov, Frédéric Pignon, Mark Rashid, Stormy May, Carolyn Resnick and Chuck Mintzlaff.

New generation
Yet Hempfling and these well-known individuals are not the only people whom I have looked to for guidance on how to become the kind of human a horse seeks to be with. Around the world there is a new generation of young horse people who are taking the lessons of the pioneers whom I have mentioned and are refashioning them in the language of the youth. I look at humans such as Noora Ehnqvist

of Finland, Jason Alexander Wauters of Belgium, Eva Roemaat here in the Netherlands and Cloé Lacroix, the Canadian dean of Nevzorov Haute Ecole to mention but a few, and it fills me with hope to see these young horse people proclaim a new standard for interaction with our equine friends. It is a standard that is based on a commitment to love, care for and be a guide to horses and their carers. In short, it is one that seeks to help people to become the kind of human a horse seeks to be with.

As you read...
It is my hope that the story, musings, mistakes and minor successes which are documented in these pages may in some small way help to make your journey towards this goal just a little bit easier. If this occurs in just one instance, it will have all been worth it.

Andrew-Glyn Smail
The Netherlands
31 October 2014

The Forest Garden, Death and a Carrot
9 January 2013

So you have decided to live intuitively. You try to tune into what is presumably your destiny by observing the signs in and around you. Now is the time to do so, for the world is counting down to a new year. First you get an urge to take up a long-standing invitation to visit a distant paradise. On the eve of your departure you send out a New Year's greeting featuring a carrot. Shortly after that you hear of the potentially impending death of a human you care for. Soon after your arrival you receive news of the death of a horse you once connected with. The signs are there: a forest garden, death and a carrot. The new year has begun. I look at this lot and shake my head. What to make of it all?

Forest Garden
Many months ago a fellow whom I met (virtually, that is) through this blog invited me to visit him in northern Portugal. I was tempted and intrigued but kept putting it off, a move facilitated in part by the topsy-turvy goings-on at our livery yard and the demands of our translation business. Ian and I seemed to have much in common. Getting on in years, both of us are former teachers of English to foreign language learners, we appreciate good music and literature, we are drawn to the Portuguese language, we embrace nature, we have only discovered a love of horses fairly recently, and we are on a journey of self-discovery through our interaction with and care for our equine friends. I was intrigued by the coincidences and tempted by the opportunity to explore them.

As we headed into the final week of the year, I felt a keen urge to take up Ian's invitation and succumbed. A total of three and a half hours of active travel later (not counting the time spent queuing, waiting, and doing what you do when you creatively queue and wait)

Contents

I found myself driving down narrow, hilly country lanes at the south-western tip of Portugal's Trás-os-Montes region in the cold, early dark of a winter's night with nothing but trust in Google Maps to guide me. Getting directions to a point tapped on a map on a smartphone is technology's equivalent of a godsend when your satellite navigation system does its equivalent of throwing up its hands in despair. And so I arrived at Forest Garden Estate, where Ian and his wife, Victoria (not sure where she got the name, because she is iconically Portuguese in almost every respect), soon had me fed, watered and warmly welcomed.

The wait until morning before I could view the estate and meet its other inmates was worth it. Banally listed as a 22-acre property, the photographs on Ian's website do not do justice to this patch of earthly paradise. Cassius, a friendly 12-year-old Sheltie, served as my partly deaf guide around the estate first thing in the morning. (Well, he guided my awareness of the terrain over which he pattered between the trees and plants, while I dictated his direction with the odd encouraging call.) Picture, if you will, a collection of intersecting trails that lead you up and down a tree-strewn hill and grassy plant-lined terraces at varying levels, some widening to become granite-buttressed fields or vineyards, while others are host to the growing collection of plants and shrubs which Ian has planted over the years. All are tucked together by a babbling stream replete with waterfalls, which half-moons around the lower section of the estate. Forest Garden Estate: the name is apt.

Impending death
On the last day of the year Vicki and I sent out New Year's greetings to friends and family in the form of a self-made online card. It features our horses proclaiming the joy of life and urging our fellow humans to enjoy it.

In reply we received an email from treasured friends in New Zealand that one of their daughters was on life support in intensive care following an attack of sepsis. One moment she was celebrating Christmas and enjoying the festive season in good health with them.

The next moment she was rushed to the local hospital and then flown to intensive care in the country's capital. The prognosis was not good as one organ after the next threatened to shut down. Not much imagination is required to conclude that our New Year's message would probably not have been deemed to be appropriate. Impending death has the tendency to eclipse life … if we let it.

Death

The morning after my arrival in Portugal I fielded a call for Vicki from her friend, Sabine, in Germany. I had only met Sabine once, when she and her husband, Frank, played host to us during our visit to Germany in March last year. You can read about our visit in my post entitled *Snippets Germane to Germany* (in *In Search for the Master Who Dances with Horses: Challenge*). Sabine was clearly disconcerted and in a hurry but I did not probe. Later that day I learned that they had been up until about five o'clock in the morning nursing Frank's horse, Pam. The mare had suddenly developed botulism the day before and had to be put down within 24 hours. The loss must be devastating.

I have a photograph of a man and a horse. The man is standing next to the horse reaching under her neck to cup her right cheek with his hand. Although the horse is looking ahead it is clear from her eyes that she is with the man as much as he is with her. The man is Frank, the horse is Pam, and they have just met closely for the first time during our visit to the livery yard that was home to Sabine's horse, Smella, at the time. Shortly after our visit Frank and Pam took each other as lawfully paired horse and human.

The loss that is death claws heavily at the heart. It is so coldly, unrelentingly final. Or so it can sometimes seem at the time. I have a large canvas picture of my dog, The Smudge, hanging on my office wall. The photo was taken when he was two years old. He died a little short of 15. Put another way, The Smudge of the picture was dead almost 13 years before I laid what had become of him since into the subtropical earth of his final resting place. I may lament The Smudge's demise but I rejoice that I am capable of doing so, for the sadness of his death is merely indicative of the joy of his life, one that I was very privileged to share. Death is the price we pay for the joy of living. The only question we are called upon to answer is whether we deem it worthwhile. It is a question we get to answer throughout our lives, either in the affirmative or the negative. The choice is ours.

The horses
And after that mini-sermon it is time to return to Forest Garden Estate, where I get to meet Gertrude Stein II, the cat, and Ian's horses, and to hear how he came to be with them. Until about four years ago Ian had virtually little or nothing to do with horses. Having two daughters, there was a pretty good chance that such a situation would change, and it did. Two mares made their way to the forest garden, one being a 15-year-old Lusitano called Lucy with a massive undeterminable growth along her right jawline, which does not seem to bother her, and the other a two-year-old cross with a French breed dubbed Doll. Lucy carried a gift with her in the form of a black filly born in April 2010, who was christened Frida. By that stage Sebastian, a two-year-old grey Lusitano stallion, had arrived. His courtship of the adult mares led to Lucy suffering a stillborn and Doll giving birth to a lovely precocious filly named Gretel in May 2011.

And so it came to pass that Ian went from no to five horses within less than five years. His equine education has consequently proceeded through immersion rather than tuition and, as in the case of all who are serious about their horsey friends, is an ongoing process. The daughters have since left the parental roost and Ian finds himself constantly but refreshingly challenged to be the best human his horses could hope for. If I was a Portuguese horse, I would be queuing up for entry into Forest Garden Estate.

According to Michael Bevilacqua, "Understanding and trust have nothing to do with training." The relationship between Ian and his horses epitomises this. During my stay I watched them interact with each other both as care-giver and receiver, and as playmates. There were moments in the round pen when I thought to myself that, if anyone with some experience of horse training were to stand there and watch Ian interacting with Lucy and Doll, they might be tempted to shake their head in scorn. Yet despite the confusion which the horses clearly experienced, they remained entirely connected to their human even after the gate was opened and they were free to go. The bond which Ian enjoys with Sebastian is also special. Horse and human can walk at liberty together. When I compare this to the difficulty which some of the World Equestrian and Olympic Games gold medal winners have merely walking their horses on a lead, I am convinced that Ian and his equine friends share a special bond with each other, one that many if not most who are proficient in horse training (whatever that may mean) can only dream of.

Life

The night before I was due to leave Portugal good news arrived from New Zealand. Not only had our young friend recovered consciousness and her reliance on life support machines been significantly reduced, she was also capable of humour and of relating fascinating stories of where her being had been while absent from her body. Life had returned and is now offering her a second chance at it, something that most of us will never have.

I look again at the online New Year's greeting which we had sent to our friends and family. It shows Pip and Anaïs peering out over the door to the indoor manège at our livery yard (hence the halters – they are not allowed to be loose). Below a photograph of the two mares there is a text purporting to be a message from them speaking the following greeting on our behalf: "On behalf of our humans, Andrew and Vicki, may we offer you these words of horse wisdom for 2013: life is a carrot … enjoy it!" The young New Zealand woman is someone whom I have known since she was six years old. I have a photograph of her as a child in a blue satin dress with her arms wrapped around our dogs. They are sharing a moment of joy, the human and the dogs. The little girl is radiant and hovers between the animals like a protective fairy. If she were to become a horse, not in appearance but in essence, life might become a carrot again.

And so it goes

And so we come full circle: the forest garden, death and a carrot. What to make of it all? Nothing. There is no need. To quote a horse I know, "Life is a carrot!" Just take a bite … and then another … and after that another … relishing each one as you go….

Stillness in the Brumby's Breath
27 February 2013

Since my visit to Ian and his horses at the beginning of the year, I have found myself frequently reflecting on the changing relations between horses and humans, especially the type of humans involved. By all accounts there is a surge in the numbers of humans who are actively seeking a relationship with horses which is one of friendship and, as such, is based on *mutual* trust and understanding. A growing number of these humans are relatively new to horses and are as unsure as to how to relate to them, as a wild Australian brumby taking its first cautious steps amongst humans. And yet we humans are so tempted to act, to do anything straightaway, even if we genuinely believe it is in the horse's best interests. Perhaps we can learn from the brumby as it stands there looking at us, guardedly to be sure, but there it remains calm and still, breathing and waiting to see what the human will do.

The numbers
In the past year I have seen the readership of this blog triple. In addition to the comments which some readers leave in response to the various posts, Vicki and I also regularly receive emails from readers scattered across the globe. Some are from friends. Most are from people whom we have never met from countries relatively close by here in Europe but also from as far afield as Australia, Pakistan, South Africa, Brazil and the United States of America to mention a few.

Most of the humans who contact us have not been interacting with horses for very long or have only been doing so on and off over the years. Some do not even have a horse of their own. Yet all are fascinated by horses and what they allow us to learn not only about our equine friends but also about ourselves and the kind of humans we would like to be.

A comment from afar

Every once in a while an email comes our way which I feel an urgent need to share with our readers. One such message recently came from a young woman called Jade in Western Australia. This email was preceded by a comment left on our blog just after Christmas in response to my post entitled *Finding Joy in the Land of Hairy Bicycles*. I am repeating it here:

Dear Andrew and Vicky,

I have been following this blog since you both started writing it and I have learned so much in the process. I have also been following Eva and Jesse since they started putting videos on YouTube and I would say that reading this blog and watching their videos has kept me going with my young horse even when I felt I wasn't right for him. About a year ago I had never ridden, been around or even remotely had anything to do with horses. One day a friend of mine took me on a trail ride at a riding school and I instantly fell in love. About a month later I looked into leasing a horse so I could learn to ride and do what I thought you had to do if you had horses (ride them every day/lunge them endlessly/put shoes on/a bit in their mouth etc.). I met Cisco, my 5yo Andalusian cross gelding, and everything changed. He taught me very quickly that the conventional way to be with horses wasn't for me or him, I did not want to train him to be a robot and he did not want to be a robot. When I first leased him he was very stubborn, very pushy, even a bit dangerous when he really disagreed with you. So, naturally, I bought him. About 3 months and several agistment centres [livery yards] later he and I found the perfect place to settle in. It's now a few more months later lives in a 30 acre paddock with several paddock mates and is very happy. We go for several walks, play together in the massive arena and he gets regular body work to keep him feeling good. We are in a good place. He will never have shoes on or a bit in his mouth again and our relationship will always be based on love and respect for each other.

I am mostly writing this now because in the last week I was involved in a brumby rescue and now have found myself with another horse. Dougie is a 2 year old brumby colt. He is a chestnut awkward-looking gangly thing and he is beautiful! Because of the similar timing to when I got Cisco, I now feel like my journey is starting all over again. I just wanted to let you know that I am so glad that people like you two and your blog and Eva and her videos to follow because it makes the journey a little less daunting and a lot more exciting and clear.

Thank you so much for posting your wisdom online!

Jade

This comment stopped me in my tracks and it did so essentially for two reasons. Firstly, it was left by someone who is relatively new to horses. And secondly, its content breathed spontaneous wisdom. Think about it. Jade essentially says the following:

1. until about a year ago she had absolutely nothing to do with horses;
2. she was smitten with horses from the very first encounter;
3. she wanted to learn to interact with horses the way convention currently dictates that we should;
4. her horse objected to that;
5. but she kept going with her young horse "even when I felt that I wasn't right for him";
6. she instinctively decided to listen to her horse and learn from him;
7. horse and human share time doing what is good for both of them.

I am utterly amazed to note that Jade has adopted an approach towards interaction with horses, which has taken some of us a great deal of time and tears to move to. She has managed to do so, I believe, because she has come to horses without the baggage of the conventional practice of humans in their efforts to impose their will on the horse. Jade has relied on instinct and intuition instead. This is something I have also seen in others who are relatively new to horses or who have come to interact with them by relying more on their instincts and intuition than conventional "wisdom".

The email

A few weeks later the email came and I just knew that I had to share it with you. Jade has kindly consented to this.

Hello Vicki and Andrew!

I commented on your blog a few weeks ago, explaining how reading your blog had helped me and my horse Cisco and how I will be getting lots of inspiration from it with my new brumby rescue colt, Dougie! I just wanted to show you what you have helped with, especially since you have introduced your horses to everyone who reads your blog. It's only fair that once in a while someone introduces their horses in return!

The first picture is of my Andalusian cross Welsh Pony, Cisco, on one of our various walks out on the roads of rural Western Australia. I had not had the idea to take Cisco for walks until I read that you did it with your mares and how it helped your relationship. I love walks with Cisco because not only does he love being out and about, but it gives us the opportunity to work together as a partnership as we decide where to go next, where to stop, how to get over and through various obstacles. Lately it has been very hot in WA, almost 2 weeks of full 40 degree weather! This means Cisco and I haven't been walking or working together as much. As with every situation, there are positive and negatives to this. The negative being that I don't see him as much, the positive being that I have been given an opportunity to spend a lot more much needed time with Dougie.

The second photo is of Dougie and the beautiful QH stallion he is paddocked with, Rebel. In this photo Rebel is affectionately resting his head on Dougie's neck, a common sight to see when they are seen together. Dougie is my 2 year old Brumby colt. He was 1 of 8 horses rescued from a property that had wild horses running on it. The rescue was organised when the property promptly had to be sold and the new owners way of deal with the horses would have been to shoot them. Most of the other horses were either mares or geldings except for Dougie, a colt, and herd leader Sarge, a 5 year old stallion. The other horses were quickly found homes but unfortunately no one seemed to want to take on an unhandled colt and stallion. Eventually they went to a lady that had her heart in the right place, but she really didn't have the experience or means to take care of them. That's where I came in. I donated wormers and my time to help with handling. It went well for a while but it soon became apparent that the boys were going to need to find new homes. The owners of my agistment centre ended up with Sarge the stallion and I ended up with Dougie. Both boys have beautiful temperaments and an amazing ability to learn! This all happened about a month ago and both have come very far. Dougie took to domestic life very quickly and loves people, he is very curious! He was castrated 2 days ago so at the moment we are focusing on getting him healed up and healthy before moving on to other things like doing his feet and teeth.

Sarge is taking a lot longer to adjust. He still doesn't trust humans and has not been comfortable enough to be touched yet except for brief forehead pats which are always on his terms. His owner and I are spending lots of quiet time with him to get used to humans and their quirky ways, which is helping a lot! His owner also is doing a bit of clicker training with him to get him used to ropes and halters. He loves his lessons so much he calls for his owner if she doesn't come on time!

The third picture I have sent you is just one of the ways we spend time with Sarge. In this photo I am reading a Mark Rashid book and relaxing with Sarge in his stall. When I first started helping out with Dougie and Sarge I found myself reading through your blogs over and over and writing down all the different bits of information and authors I could look up that I thought might help. Mark Rashid has been a big one for me, especially his non-confrontational way of communicating with horses. I am going through all of his books at the moment and it has helped immensely! Especially with my perspective on working with horses and even life itself.

You two will never know how much reading your blog has helped me with my approach with my horses. If you don't believe me, just ask Cisco and Dougie!

I hope both your beautiful mares are going very well and that the sticky situation with your livery is getting sorted out! I would love to know more about your mares and where your journey is at the moment, if you ever feel like you want to talk about it.

Thanks so much,

Jade

In a follow-up email accompanying her photos Jade writes:

When I first got Dougie to the agistment centre, I would do short regular training sessions to get him ready for being gelded and lots of handling. One day we were in the middle of a session and Dougie decided to drop down and go to sleep! After this photo was taken he laid flat out and started to snore. I was very honoured that he was comfortable enough to sleep around me.

My reply

The reason why I have shared this email with you is because it deals with what I believe is the key to connecting with horses and ultimately to coming to terms with who we are with or without the horse. This I consider in my reply to Jade.

Dear Jade

It is heart-warming to hear that our blog is helping humans, such as you, to find their way to horses, such as Cisco and Dougie. Ultimately though, we are just as much on a journey with our horses as you and other humans are with theirs.

The only difference though is that we put it all "out there", as it were. Some of it is disappointing, devastating, heart-wrenching and sometimes simply downright embarrassing. Other parts of it are exhilarating, soothing, inspiring and sometimes simply utterly nurturing. At the end of it all though, it is simply what it is. And this is all that matters.

Intuitively knowing

At present I am reading a book by Linda Kohanov called The Tao of Equus. It is a book that we have carried around with us on our wanderings for some six years but it is only now that I have felt ready to read it, and I am glad I waited, because it rewardingly intellectualises (a process required for understanding as opposed to knowing) what is ultimately the very straightforward process of being (and through that intuitively knowing).

It seems to me that in your interaction with Cisco and Dougie you have not so much applied what you feel that you have learned through our blog as you have instinctively sought to find a way of simply being with your horses in a way that is beneficial to both you and them. You have intuitively known what to do by observing your horses and tapping in to your own wellspring of empathy and empowerment. Their trust in you is evidence of that. What you have read through us and the guides whom we refer to has simply helped you to flesh out the approach that you and your horses had already embarked on. Take confidence in that, for it is yours.

Escape and evasion

It is probably because of this that your young brumby, Dougie, has taken to domestic life and humans very quickly, whereas his wild mate, Sarge, is taking a lot longer to adjust. In her book Linda Kohanov makes the point that, "As a prey animal, a horse simply isn't giving his full attention to the lesson when he feels threatened; he's figuring out how to escape" (p. 151). Although she was referring specifically to the phenomenon of horses resorting to evasion while being trained, the awareness of a perceived threat and the urgent need to escape it represent a primeval instinct for survival which is at the forefront of life in the wild.

Nature may be beautiful but it can also be uncompromisingly hard, particularly in the conditions in which the wild brumbies of Australia live. Add human intervention to the mix in the form of regular culling expeditions (many if not most of which are barbarous to the extreme) and it comes as no surprise that brumbies are predominantly guided by their survival instinct.

Connecting

So how do you go about connecting with a horse that is preoccupied with the need to survive? Klaus Ferdinand Hempfling insists that trust-nurturing dominance is required in the human. The theory is that, if the human is dominant, the horse will no longer have a reason to fear and can trust the human to ensure its survival and look after its needs. This trust will help create the bond required for horse and human to connect with each other. The problem with this approach is that it works with some horses but not with others. Indeed, evidence is available to suggest that it has the potential to create a "dangerous" horse.

You have also mentioned that Sarge, the untrusting brumby, is responding well to clicker training. I am not an expert on clicker training and therefore do not feel capable of commenting on it. However, I would question – and I use this term in its literal sense as opposed to an expression of doubt – its value firstly with regard to the nature of the connection it creates between horse and human. Is the connection that it produces purely mechanical or does it facilitate the sharing of a constantly interactive flow of sensory energy which is so typical of a magical or true connection? Secondly, what type of horse does it ultimately produce: a conditioned robot or a genuine willing partner in full control of its faculties. Put another way, is clicker training empathetic and empowering?

Another approach

There is another approach and that is simply to allow the horse to be in conditions which are safe and comforting, allowing the human to become part of this to the extent that the horse permits and encourages this. As the horse settles down in his daily routine, the human can increasingly become part of this by simply sharing space with the horse. Carolyn Resnick employs this approach as part of her "waterhole rituals" and one of her students, Stina Herberg, has used it to good effect as part of the process of rehabilitating and training a herd of feral horses at her home on a Caribbean island.

In January 2007 Herberg took on the surviving seven of an original herd of 16 former racehorses from Barbados which had been sold as 'riding horses' en route to the slaughterhouse. They had gone feral, were malnourished and were very distrustful of humans.

Of methods and replication

Stina Herberg learned a great deal from Carolyn Resnick and is very grateful to her for her input and inspiration. Not only does she recommend Resnick to others but she has also become a certified Carolyn Resnick instructor. In The Tao of Equus Linda Kohanov warns of the dangers of following a method and attempting to replicate a trainer who is as intrinsically innovative in the use of her method as Resnick herself. However, the fact that she is, is no guarantee that her students and certified instructors will also be intuitively creative. Indeed, marketing a method and replicating a mode of instruction are processes which inherently militate against intuition, creativity and innovation.

Writing of methods and replication, Linda Kohanov has this to say and I quote it with wholehearted consent (although I must confess to having misgivings about the use of the term, "equestrians"):

> Most of these methods work because they were created from a responsive, innovative state of awareness. If this mindset is discouraged in the apprentice, how can he or she truly represent the essence of the clinician's vision? The notion of The Method capable of automatically giving anyone who follows it the powers of an innovative trainer must give way to dedicated equestrians willing to support each other in exploring the ethical, experiential, emotional, sociosensual, and intuitive qualities that bring those methods to life. (p. 177)

Put another way, the notion of being anyone's certified instructor should yield to an acknowledgement that all trainers worthy of the title have as unique and innovative an approach as those from whom they learn.

The Herberg approach

Fortunately, Herberg appears to have developed her own approach. Although she is nominally a certified Carolyn Resnick instructor, it is clear that Herberg is anything but a method practitioner or a Resnick clone. The following video is a case in point. Although it pointedly recommends Carolyn Resnick at the end, you would be hard put to find anything in that trainer's repertoire of videos which coincides with this one. And so it should be for both are unique, even though they share much in common as good trainers do.

Having said that, the Herberg video which I would like to leave you with is one which ostensibly applauds "The Carolyn Resnick Method" but actually celebrates not only a very important part of that method but of any meaningful interaction between horses and humans: having fun just being together and in doing so, building understanding and trust. I keep going back to this quote but it cannot be said often enough: "Understanding and trust have nothing to do with training." Amen and thank you, Michael Bevilacqua. You can view the video at http://www.youtube.com/watch?v=J2hf5cq03XE.

Congruence and authenticity

Where we humans differ from horses in terms of our immediate interaction with our surroundings and the creatures that inhabit them, lies in our ability to become incongruent or inauthentic. As Linda Kohanov points out:

> In horses it appears that memories are stimulated by emotion and the physiological sensations that give rise to those emotions. However, these animals do not actually separate thought and memory from feeling and sensation. The four are always connected. (This is why an action like lowering the head will calm a frightened horse.) (p. 162)

Unlike horses, humans are capable of differentiating thought and memory from feeling and sensation. We are more inclined to define ourselves according to what we think and remember rather than what we feel and sense. Where the sensory and the cognitive coincide, we are congruent or authentic. Where they do not, we are incongruent or inauthentic.

Put in everyday terms, if you are going through a particularly stressful patch at home or work and you allow your mental preoccupation with it to override what you would like to feel and sense in the moment when you go to your horse, you will be perceived to be incongruent and inauthentic by your horse. Mutually beneficial interaction between horse and human will become difficult if not impossible.

The physiology of stress

Whether a horse is wild (like the Przewalskis or Asian wild horses), feral (such as the American mustangs or Australian brumbies) or domestic, there is always a little bit of brumby in it. Yet its survival instinct and the fear it begets in threatening conditions is something that is not unique to the horse. It is something that we can find in the human as well.

Referring to what she calls the "physiology of stress", Kohanov quotes a study which "concludes that particularly traumatic or repetitive stressful experiences in childhood actually shape the brain's structure". She goes on to state:

> The brain develops by creating circuitry patterns in response to experience. Severely abused children, to use the most extreme example, consistently associate the feeling of stress with negative, even life-threatening outcomes. Unless this pattern is counteracted and other brain pathways are created, these people continue to respond to the slightest sense of pressure or uncertainty as an emergency, immediately falling into the flight, fight or freeze mode. (p. 152)

This sounds very much like the condition of a wild horse trying to survive in conditions where it is next in line in some other creature's food chain. Indeed, some of us have even come across a less acute version of this phenomenon in domestic horses that have been abused. And it does not take much to abuse a horse. It can be as simple as leaving a horse in a stable for far too long every day. Even those humans amongst us who have not been severely abused as a child may be able to recognise a mild version of this primeval fear in the seemingly incessant worrying that characterises our waking moments.

Embracing the brumby

The challenge lies in embracing the brumby in us and accepting it for what it is, a fear which in almost every case has absolutely no basis in the reality of the moment in which we currently find ourselves. To do this we are not called upon to succumb to this fear by making it the constant subject of our conscious thought. Instead, we are challenged to reunite our consciousness with our feelings and sensory awareness of the here and now, to the point that all we become conscious of is the moment in which we find ourselves to the exclusion of everything that has no place in that moment. In this way we can make our thoughts congruent with our sensory and emotional awareness, and by so doing rediscover the authenticity of the self.

This is the challenge of the horse when we enter its presence. As Kohanov puts it, "A mind tuned to embrace the entire body – while connecting socio-sensually with the body-mind of the horse – is the key to equine success" (p. 165). Essentially, it is not about us but about the horse yet, ultimately, it is through the horse that we can rediscover some of our lost self. Kohanov is almost poetic in her conclusion:

> Even mortal horses can lead people to secret springs of lost knowledge, and they're fully capable of carrying the living dead, those lobotomised by the current paradigm, to a hidden realm of emotional and creative vitality, a kingdom that is within us all. (p. 166)

Jade, together with your horses, you seem to be well on the way to discovering that kingdom within you. May all of you journey safely together!

Be well!
Andrew

21

Stillness

There he is, standing there looking at us, waiting to see what the human will do. And what the brumby sees, intrigues him, for the human does nothing or at least nothing directed against the horse. The brumby turns back to its pasture. And so they pass the time, horse and human, together but apart. Then the human leaves and the brumby returns to its grazing. The next day the scenario is repeated and the day after that and so on until the human's visits become routine. The horse becomes accustomed to the human and tolerates their presence, until one day the brumby succumbs to curiosity and approaches the human. So there they stand, the horse's breath gently caressing the human's hair. And in the horse's breath the human discovers stillness. The precursor to the dance has begun.

A Path … to the Horse … to the Human
17 March 2013

In the past few months Vicki and I have embarked on yet another path to the horse, one that has led me to contemplate all the other paths that we have followed, and which have ultimately brought us full circle to the human whom we aspire to be. Before devoting a post to this, I would like to look back to where it all began for us in Australia when we discovered Alexander Nevzorov and soon after Klaus Ferdinand Hempfling. What really captured my imagination at the time was not only the apparent prowess of these "masters" – after all, it is what one expects of them – but also the story of just another ordinary human – persecuting horses in the way that many of us learned to do – who experienced an epiphany of awareness. The result was, is and has been dramatically liberating … for that human, her horses, me, and other horses and humans around the world. Now, some five years on, I would like to revisit this ongoing story with you.

From answers to questions
If America is the country where dreams meet success, she was just another epitome of this stereotype. As a child she developed a passion for horses. She dreamt of filling her life with horses and she succeeded. She decided to become a horse trainer and she succeeded, if the number of trained horses that left her stable was anything to go by. She decided to become a riding instructor and she succeeded, if the number of reasonably accomplished riders who left her training centre was anything to go by. Indeed, so successful was she, that she was admitted into the ranks of the equestrian establishment as a competition judge.

This young woman had all the answers about horses for those humans who sought her assistance. Yet something was missing.

Somewhere along the way the paths of the human and her horse had separated. True, she had her horse and he did what his human demanded of him. But where was the horse of her dreams, the noble creature with whom she had once aspired to dance? She looked back at pictures of her childhood with horses and asked herself, "Where had the beauty, majesty and freedom of horses gone?" And what had happened to the human who had found beauty in those childhood dreams? As she puts it:

> I used to be a horse trainer. I used to be a riding instructor ... until the day I realised that somewhere I had gone off course.

In search of answers

So the young woman looked around her for answers. Her search brought her into contact with the films and writings of people who seemed to have discovered the elusive horse-human relationship of her dreams. They have since become household names to a growing number of humans who are actively searching for a new way of being with horses: Mark Rashid, Linda Kohanov, Carolyn Resnick, Klaus Ferdinand Hempfling and Alexander Nevzorov. "These people broke with tradition and focused more on what we can learn from horses than what we can teach them." And so the young woman decided to go and speak to these people.

The Path of the Horse

The young woman's name was Stormy May. She used her video camera to produce a documentary of her search for answers, which she called *The Path of the Horse*. Vicki and I saw it soon after it was released and arranged a screening of it for "horsey" friends in our home outside Byron Bay. We subsequently learned that we were but a small number of the humans who have been so profoundly challenged by that film to follow the path of the horse.

> I made a choice to leave behind the life I knew. I sold my ranch to fund this search, bought a video camera and plane tickets and set out to find a different way of doing things.

Five years on, Stormy May has decided to release *The Path of the Horse* for all of us to view free of charge. If you have never seen this documentary before, it comes highly recommended. Those of us who have seen it may wish to view it again, if only to dip into some of the energy that inspired us to travel the path we are on. You can view it at http://www.youtube.com/watch?v=TQUMAJCh1fA.

The path to *Our Horses*

Since embarking on her path to the horse and ultimately to the human within her, Stormy May has found a home for herself and her horses in northern California, one where horse and human can live side-by-side without either making demands on the other. Here they can help each other discover what it means to be fully horse and fully human.

As an extension of this Stormy May has linked up with like-minded humans around the world to establish an international community called *Our Horses*. Its mission statement is disarmingly unpretentious:

> We are an international community of friends working together to create a better world starting with providing sanctuary for horses and humans. We are dedicated to spreading peace through heart and feeling-based education with horses at our sanctuaries and by working together on service projects that uplift humanity.

Horse and human sanctuaries

At the time of writing *Our Horses* lists seven horse and human sanctuaries on its website. There are four in the United States of America: two in California, one in Wisconsin and one in Texas. The latter is headed by Brandy and Ren, a gifted photographer and dedicated barefoot trimmer whom Vicki and I were privileged to meet at the Nevzorov Haute Ecole seminar hosted by Michael Bevilacqua and Chloe Lacroix in Canada in September last year (see my post entitled *At the Interface of Horse-Human Interaction*).

Europe is also represented. There is an Our Horses sanctuary in Poland, another in Denmark and a third in north-eastern Spain (or

Catalonia depending on your point of view). Perhaps more will come, not only in Europe but also in other parts of the world.

Online community

Our Horses includes an online community which is open to anyone who shares the commitment expressed in the Our Horses mission statement. Here members from around the world can network with each other, sharing ideas and helping each other.

The online community has spawned a number of groups with a specific focus. One of these is the "hontonto relationships" group. The information provided about this group mentions that "hontonto" is "a Maidu Indian word meaning together in heart and spirit, used to designate a way of being with horses and others that is characterized by freedom from force, restriction, and pain and focused on healing and leading healthy lives in community".

Uplifting commitment

The hontonto relationships group represents an uplifting commitment to improving the lives of horses and humans. The members of this group make the following pledge:

OurHorses pledge

I pledge to create peaceful, healthy, hontonto relationships with the horses in my life. While I cannot know for certain how a horse experiences being ridden, scientific studies have shown that riding can cause pain and damage to a horse's back, head, mouth, and other parts of their bodies. I will not ride, nor will I support equestrian sport, which places human gratification over the well-being of horses.

I pledge to not breed horses or condone the breeding of captive horses while there are not enough homes for all the horses alive today to live lives where they are protected and cared for.

I pledge to use the time that would be spent riding or in other self-serving pursuits to heal myself, so I can help care for others and the planet we share. I will spend less time in ways that gratify primarily myself or my immediate family, (e.g.

television watching, gaming, sports, travel, shopping, hobbies, etc.) and devote the resources that would have been spent on these to help create and support sanctuaries for horses and humans where everyone is cared for.

I pledge to use my gifts and talents to share what I have in excess with my neighbours and my family from all parts of the world in the best ways I know how according to my heart stirrings.

Uplifting challenge

The hontonto relationship group's *OurHorses Pledge* is the most radically uplifting challenge – that I am aware of anyway – issued to those of us humans who have chosen to spend a large part of our lives with horses. As such, not everyone will feel called upon to subscribe to it. Where its strength lies though is in the direction towards which it points. It is a path to the horse as the horse seeks to exist in its own right. And ultimately, by acknowledging the horse for what it is and helping it to be a horse rather than an accessory to the human ego, it is a path to the human waiting to be released within each one of us. Amen!

Hempfling's Student: Casting off the Master's Shadow
7 April 2013

On 20 July 2012 a young woman from Belgium walked out on Klaus Ferdinand Hempfling's first full-time one-year course after having studied with the master who dances with horses for a little over seven and a half months. She left behind not only the master himself but also her eight remaining fellow students with whom she had shared a home for so long, and a dream. On 19 March 2013 one of those students phoned an independent Belgian horse centre on behalf of Hempfling's Akedah International organisation and demanded that the centre cancel courses which were to be given there by the young woman and that the centre remove all materials advertising those courses from its website, implying that if it failed to do so legal action would be taken against it. The centre removed the advertising materials from its website and the young woman again finds herself trying to cast off the master's shadow.

The young woman
The young woman is Jasmijn Wauters, a highly gifted and sensitive facilitator of mutually rewarding interaction between horses and humans. She had encountered Hempfling through his books and videos well before she joined his one-year course in September 2011.

Jasmijn Wauters grew up amongst horses and ostriches. From the time she was a child she learned that communication is the key to working with animals. Pursuing her own inherent approach, she trained her first horse, a young stallion, called Colorado, using only body language. In 2012 Jasmijn established EDEN, which stands for *Escuela Del Equilibrio Natural* and represents the essence of what she seeks to achieve. Her school has acquired a Spanish tint through her contact with the breeding regime of Pura Raza Española de

Estirpe Cartujana. As in all life arts, interaction with horses can teach us wisdom about life and how we humans can find or rediscover the finest version of the self within us.

The Hempfling representative
Akedah International is the Danish organisation through which Hempfling provides his courses. Hempfling exercises tight control over what is done and said through Akedah in his name. We may therefore safely assume that the person who called the Belgian centre and demanded that Jasmijn's courses be halted did so with Hempfling's full knowledge and authorisation.

Hempfling's representative in this matter is both a fellow countrywoman to Jasmijn and was a former fellow student to her during the one-year course. Her name is Cecile and she would also have been a fellow student to Vicki and myself, if Hempfling had not thrown us out of his one-year course. In fact, Vicki actually attended Hempfling's Compact Schooling 1 course with Cecile in 2010.

The demand
Obviously Cecile must have stayed on in Denmark after the unfinished one-year course to help Hempfling run his operations. Being Belgian and a Flemish speaker, it must have seemed entirely logical for Cecile to be assigned the task of calling the Belgian centre in Flanders to demand that Jasmijn's courses be cancelled and that the advertising materials for those courses be removed from the centre's website.

The rationale for this demand lay in an accusation made by Hempfling's representative to the effect that at some stage the advertising materials for Jasmijn's courses had contained claims insinuating more than the facts concerning Jasmijn's studies with Hempfling. Apparently, this was no longer the case when Cecile called but she insisted, that because students had been recruited on that premise, the courses should be cancelled.

The response

The Belgian centre which Hempfling's representative called is Aneto Foresta in Mol, just a hop, skip and a jump across the Belgian border not too far from where we live in the south of the Netherlands. To all intents and purposes Aneto Foresta is a stranger to Hempfling and Akedah International, although Hempfling does feature as one of the organisation's sources of inspiration.

Understandably, Aneto Foresta was concerned about an accusation such as this being made by one of the organisation's sources of inspiration. If Hempfling was to take legal action, what impact would that have on the organisation's business?

The facts

After Jasmijn abandoned Hempfling's one-year course, she returned to Belgium, where she started to teach, offering assistance to humans looking for a new way of interacting with horses through her school, EDEN (Escuela Del Equilibrio Natural). As part of her teaching activities, Jasmijn and EDEN arranged to offer some courses through Aneto Foresta's centre.

Soon after the original advertising materials appeared on the Aneto Foresta website, they were updated to reflect no more than some of the bald facts of Jasmijn's experience, which includes her two stints with Hempfling in Denmark. And the facts of Jasmijn's Hempfling experience are as follows:

- she studied Hempfling's approach towards horses through his books and videos;
- she attended Hempfling's Pure Practical Performance course in 2010;
- during the period from September 2011 to July 2012 she spent a total of a little over seven and a half months attending a full-time course with Hempfling along with nine other students, which was supposed to last 12 months but by the time of writing had not gone beyond the tenth month;

- during her studies with Hempfling she worked with three different stallions, which she had taken with her to his school;
- she was the only student who regularly worked with a stallion during her studies with Hempfling, as the latter took over the training of the only other stallion available during the one-year course (Habanero, the small, black stallion owned by Hempfling's senior body awareness coach, Jo Ross);
- she was only one of two of the one-year students whom Hempfling felt were good enough to feature briefly in one of the numerous videos which he published on YouTube during the one-year course.

These are the facts of Jasmijn's studies with Hempfling and in as much as they have helped to define her approach towards helping humans be with horses, she would be shirking her responsibility to mention her defining influences (which include Hempfling) if she failed to include at least some of them in her publicity materials. In this, she is not unique. Many if not most trainers acknowledge their defining influences in their professional profile. To suggest that Jasmijn is implying anything more by mentioning them is to play loose with the truth.

Ignorance and fear
Given that Jasmijn's few references to her defining Hempfling influences in her advertising materials for her Aneto Foresta courses were unembellished facts, why then did the organisation remove them from its website after Hempfling's representative demanded that it do so? To be sure, it had a legitimate concern for its business but there were more important issues at stake.

Aneto Foresta felt that it had become embroiled in a dispute which was not of its making and which essentially had nothing to do with it. Clearly this was a dispute between Akedah and Hempfling, on the one hand, and Jasmijn, on the other. Akedah and Hempfling were simply trying to prevent Jasmijn from earning a living through any horse-human training whose advertising materials included a professional profile of the trainer which contained any reference to either of them, but they did not dare to take action against her directly. Is it because they were aware that such action might unlawfully prejudice her rights or that it might contravene European competition law? This time Akedah and Hempfling tackled Jasmijn through Aneto Foresta. Who will it be next time? ... if they dare.

Ultimately though, Aneto Foresta had a choice. Instead of removing the advertising materials for Jasmijn's courses as Hempfling's representative demanded, it could have left them in place after rightfully insisting that Cecile contact Jasmijn directly. Were Akedah and Hempfling counting on Aneto Foresta to act on the basis of ignorance and fear?

David and Goliath

And what of Jasmijn? When the master sent his representative to effectively intimidate an organisation into abandoning courses which would have enabled his former student not only to earn some money through those courses but also to extend her reputation and attract more business further down the track, what effect was that designed to have on her?

In the short time that EDEN has been operating, Jasmijn has been trying to generate an income that will enable her to live independently of state or family support. And she has been trying to do this by teaching humans to interact with horses in a way that is beneficial to both horse and human. Yet here we have the single most important external defining influence on her approach, a man who is so immensely popular (as he seeks to remind us through his publicity materials by incessantly citing his Facebook Likes and YouTube view count) as to enjoy widespread authority, behaving like a veritable Goliath in relation to the David of his former student. Yet he only does so indirectly and dares not do so to her face.

Casting off the master's shadow

Late at night just hours before leaving Akedah International's one-year schooling course Jasmijn wrote an email to Hempfling in an effort to explain her decision. For numerous reasons it was a very difficult decision, because it also meant that Jasmijn was abandoning a dream which she and her father had made huge sacrifices to realise. There is a line in that email which brings tears to my eyes every time I read it, and it is this. The student writes to the master:

> It feels for me as if I am a little tree living in the shadow of a big tree – whose shadow is so great that it blocks the sunlight.

Among the many reasons why Jasmijn left Hempfling, this is the most poignant. The student sought to cast off the master's shadow. Eight months later she finds herself still trying to do so, as the master's shadow mushrooms and threatens to engulf her world in darkness.

A plea to the master

O master who dances with horses, I know that you will read this, for your trusted servant, Cecile will again alert you to what I have written, just as she did after every one of my posts featuring you during your one-year schooling course. Yes, I was amazed to hear from eye witnesses that this had occurred, as was Vicki. And we were both astounded by how often we were mentioned by you during that course and with such emphatic feeling. This must be some type of record for people who were not even in attendance.

O master who dances with horses, I fall on my knees to beg you to allow your former student, Jasmijn, to pursue her professional life while acknowledging your defining influence. She does justice to your influence probably more than any other student you have ever had. Jasmijn is the only student you have had study with you so long who worked with stallions during her studies with you and who is now actively teaching humans how to interact with stallions and other horses in a way that acknowledges the nobility of both species. More importantly, she is doing so not as a slavish, sect-like, robotic follower but as a free, independent spirit seeking to empathise and

empower horses and humans, and through this to achieve enlight–
enment. And she is doing this while acknowledging your defining
influence.

> O master, please cut off the branch that casts such a long,
> dark shadow!

Our Horses Banished by the Ice Queen
14 May 2013

When the celebrations following the inauguration of the Netherlands' first king in 120 years descended into the calm of the early hours of May, only two client horses remained munching on their straw bedding in our livery yard. Little did they suspect that they would not spend another night in those stables. The Ice Queen, who has wielded power in our livery yard since she assumed the role of tenant a year earlier, had decreed that all clients were to be banished from her yard by the beginning of the month. Our horses were the last to go. And so it came to pass that later that day, after almost two years of interesting times, Andrew and Vicki led Pip and Anaïs out of the livery yard, through the adjoining forest to their new uncertain accommodation several kilometres down the road.

Queen of chaos
Some of you may be familiar with the Ice Queen, as you may have been introduced to her when she first graced the pages of this blog back in October 2012. Alternatively, you may have come across her when she again featured in a post entitled *In Search of Houyhnhnms in a Land of Hairy Bicycles* (in *In Search of the Master Who Dances with Horses: Challenge*) in December.

A vice-president with an international asset management firm serving institutional investors, the Ice Queen has done no more than live up to the stereotype of what us lesser mortals might cynically expect of such a role-player in our own back yard. She has sought only the best for herself and her 11 horses, and has been quite happy to sacrifice her staff, suppliers, clients and landlord in the process, leaving a trail of human and equine chaos in her wake.

In darkness there is light

If you have read my previous posts on the subject, you will be aware that at some stage the situation deteriorated to the extent that our horses came under threat. Their health was compromised and that was simply unacceptable. And so Vicki and I went in search of alternative accommodation, spending a few days on the road and scouring the land, ultimately to no avail. Even with the problems that we were experiencing and for which we found makeshift solutions, there was simply nothing available that could compare to what we had available for our horses at the time.

Not too long after, as the days started lengthening towards the end of the year, the pale gleam of a distant light at the end of the proverbial tunnel began to advance on us through the darkness. Having failed to develop the various equine enterprises she had envisaged for herself in the Netherlands, having failed to nurture the contacts in the Dutch equestrian establishment to which money had helped her gain access, and having failed to put down roots in the local community, the Ice Queen sought refuge where she had come from, first exiling her person from the everyday affairs of the livery yard followed by what was supposed to be the piece-by-piece removal of her horses and other possessions. Winter may have been cold on the ground but the periods of daylight were becoming noticeably longer, and not only literally as far as I was concerned.

Rediscovering balance

Towards the end of last year Vicki, who had been actively searching for a programme of activities to help Anaïs redevelop her constitution and condition, stumbled upon something called *rechtrichten* in Dutch, which its local proponents have chosen to translate as "straightness training", and which I prefer to dub "body balancing" in conjunction with complementary disciplines designed to achieve the same. Ultimately derived from the classical equestrian tradition propounded by the French masters, Antoine de Pluvinel (1552-1620) and François Robichon de La Guérinière (1668-1751), body balancing recognises that horses, like humans, are asymmet-

36

rical in their posture and gait, an acknowledgement which presupposes the need for a programme of action to remedy this.

Such a programme of action seeks to help the horse address its asymmetry by developing its muscles in such a way that it acquires balance in torso and limbs and that its centre of gravity shifts to the centre of its frame. This is particularly important where a horse is called upon to interact with its human in exertions which demand great physical and mental effort on the part of both species. Indeed, one may wish to go a step further by insisting that any body balancing programme for the horse be accompanied by one for its human. This is particularly relevant where horse and human are ultimately to interact between their back and bum respectively.

Dispelling the mythology of hardware
Unfortunately, the classical equestrian tradition got lost in the hard, harsh, taut-reined nonsense which currently passes for equestrian proficiency at the highest levels of competitive dressage. Some individuals, such as Bent Branderup in Denmark and Marijke de Jongh here in the Netherlands, are seeking to resurrect that tradition. De Jongh, in particular, stresses the potential healing effects of the "straightness training" which is inherent in that tradition.

Unfortunately, the emphasis is still placed on riding as the primary focus of these efforts coupled with the almost inevitable use of traditional hardware to realise it. Of course, the double bridle with its metal curb and snaffle in the horse's mouth, and sharp metal spurs in its side undermine the very image of an equine body in balance. After all, surely the point of equine balance is that the horse achieves it freely rather than that the human secures it with force (however "light"). Nevzorov and others have already shown that it is possible for the horse to balance and collect itself in the absence of hardware. Perhaps it is time for the proponents of "straightness training" to rethink the paradigm.

Starting out

Because we had heard that "straightness training" had really helped horses with a history of sacro-iliac joint issues (such as Anaïs), Vicki decided to embark on a programme of activity with her mare. I watched one of these sessions and was intrigued. Horse and human seemed to be involved in a subtle interplay of energy which not only brought them closer together but also appeared to benefit the horse.

It was downright inspiring to see Anaïs transformed from an at times somewhat hesitant or bolshie creature into a quizzical mare visibly endeavouring to process the subtle cues flowing her way. This big bull of a horse turned to butter. In turn, the calm of the horse transformed the human, who became more responsive to the slightest variation in equine energy. Horse and human morphed into a gliding whorl of energy.

Equine body balancing with Pip

It was clear to me from the first lesson which I witnessed from the sidelines, that "straightness training" is definitely something that could be of great benefit to Pip (any ultimately myself as well). For much of her 16 years Pip has been *dressaged* on the forehand with the bulk of her weight flowing into her right shoulder. The outcome has been an asymmetrical bend to the left with the result that her right hind leg steps significantly shorter than its counterpart on the left. The impact on her feet has also been remarkable: her right fore hoof is significantly lower on the heel and longer in the toe than the left. In the absence of remedial trimming, this very impact must in turn have reinforced the asymmetry of her movement to reduce the entire thing to a rather unpleasant vicious circle. I now fully understand why Pip often used to escape into flight, especially when called upon to canter: she was trying to evade discomfort if not pain.

Pip and I have been actively involved in body balancing since late December. The first thing I did was find a cavasson which does not have any metal flowing through the noseband, because the Marijke de Jong variant which we had does have a metal-reinforced nose–band and I refuse to use it on any horse. To me the cavasson is simply a device to facilitate communication while allowing Pip to regulate the position of her head herself (connecting through a halter tends to pull the head out of sync). The next thing I did was to tie my trimming of Pip's hooves more closely in with the exercises we share by trying to balance them almost to the point of being "unnatural". Ordinarily, I would trim Pip's hooves down to the sole proper (that is, the sole less its flaky surface), which then served as my guide. Now I have started to bring the heels of her left fore hoof as low as possible while keeping the toe as long as safety allows. Conversely, on the right fore I endeavour to cut back the toe as far as possible and leave the heels long enough to bring them into line with those of her left fore hoof. In short, I am hoping that over time a holistic approach of remedial trimming, Equine Touch and focused "straightness training" exercises will help Pip rebalance her body not only in her movement but also in the shape of her feet. It is a long-term goal and we have time on our side.

Body balancing exercises with Pip
You may be interested in some of the exercises I am doing with Pip. When we started out we were looking for regulated movement at the walk and trot as the horse starts to relearn how to use its body and find its new balance. The focus was on a combination of lateral flexion coupled with the forward and downward movement of the head and neck, allowing the horse to relax its back muscles, strengthen its abdominal ones and learn to step under its mass. If all is not well, as it usually is in the beginning, the horse will seek evasion by speeding up. Pip did so too, predictably on the right.

We have come a long way since we started. Pip has learned to combine lateral flexion, the downward and forward movement of her head and neck, and the ability to step under in a flowing move in a single direction. She finds this more difficult on the right. Much of the work that Pip and I are currently doing on the lunge involves circle work covering a variety of diameters to gymnasticise her body and help her learn to carry herself centred in her being without falling out at the extremities. She is quite capable of doing small circles on the right but her head is sometimes at odds with the direction in which she is headed. In our last lesson Pip and I learned to do shoulder-in but we still have a way to go.

Misgivings and issues
Given the background to and origins of "straightness training" along with its ultimate preoccupation with riding, I must confess to having a few misgivings about it and can foresee a number of issues arising. Perhaps the most disconcerting misgivings that I have tend to relate to the emphasis placed on guiding the head and as such, seeking to guide the horse from the front to the rear instead of vice versa, the latter being more logical an approach if self-collection is the ultimate posture and movement-related goal.

True, I can understand the logic of the horse needing to discover its authentic symmetrical balance and that, as it does so, and as its hindquarters and abdominal muscles consequently start to develop the strength and flexibility required to enable the horse to move from its core, it will ultimately start to shift more of its weight to the hindquarters and to bring up the base of its neck. To my mind, this move towards self-collection suggests that the head will find its own position and that there will consequently be a need at some point to toss out the cavasson in favour of an aid such as a cordeo around the base of the neck, for instance. It also suggests the need for a training environment in which the horse is capable of learning how to carry itself, one which has clearly discernible finite barriers, such as the walls of Nevzorov's school manège or Hempfling's picadero, until ultimately, even those will no longer be required. Whatever the case, I cannot envisage any place in this scenario for metal in the mouth or on the foot.

Of curses and blessings
The Ice Queen's banishment of our horses from their familiar surroundings has been a curse on our endeavours to help our horses through equine body balancing. Still we must be thankful to her through no fault of her own. As she has continued to alienate staff

and has consequently been abandoned by them, the number of people using the facilities in our livery yard diminished drastically. As a result Vicki and I found that in the first four months of this year, we frequently had top facilities available for us and our horses to interact with each other in the absence of anyone else. It has helped us tremendously, if the physical and mental improvement of our horses – especially Anaïs – is anything to go by.

True, our horses' banishment has put an end to this, at least for the time being. Yet there is a positive side to this as well. For about a fortnight prior to our departure from the Ice Queen's livery yard, we noticed that all of the horses in our herd (our two mares and two others) had started to lose weight. We started giving all of them additional feed but to no avail. The Ice Queen had condemned our horses to a relatively bare field for months, one in which every bit of new grass was eaten almost before it had a chance to grow. We had had a worm count done and there was no indication that we needed to worm the horses. We complained and nothing was done. Now that we are looking after our horses ourselves, we can see them piling the weight back on and they are beginning to look healthy again. This is a blessing, so too is the fact that we are looking after them ourselves. Neither Vicki or I had realised how much we missed this.

Banishment? Whose banishment?
True, not living on the same premises as our horses does have its drawbacks. There is the time involved in shunting between home and the horse facility, coupled with the inconvenience of forgetting something and not being able to run inside and get it. We console ourselves that this is a temporary solution but how long is temporary?

The Ice Queen is embroiled in a conflict with the owners of the livery yard. Matters have taken such a turn for the worse, that the owners are seeking to have the Ice Queen evicted. The matter goes to court next Tuesday afternoon. The question on everyone's lips is whether the Ice Queen and the goblins who execute her commands no matter how horse-unfriendly they may be will not in turn be banished from the livery yard next week. It will be as it will be and that will be fine. My only concern is that no horse suffer as a result. The humans can look after themselves. And now it is time to hang out with Pip again....

Horses, Humans, Hempfling and How to Get Started
18 June 2013

For the past two to three weeks I have been corresponding with someone who has been involved in ongoing discussions on Klaus Ferdinand Hempfling's official Facebook page. Although the precise nature of these discussions varies, the debate can essentially be reduced to the question of what is required of an individual to become the type of human a horse seeks to be with. It is the very question that led Vicki and myself to leave Australia in order to spend a year studying with Hempfling, one which has closely defined my own self-development since that option failed to materialise, and one which continues to inspire my posts on this blog, whose very by-line is becoming the kind of human a horse seeks to be with. So how do you start to become this type of human and what does the process entail?

One of Hempfling's answers

Since last year Klaus Ferdinand Hempfling has been maintaining a Facebook page which had attracted 378,000 *likes* (not quite members or a community, as Hempfling consistently states in his advertising materials but impressive nevertheless) by the time of writing. Whether some or many of those *likes* are bogus or not (see for example the BBC reports on fraudulent *likes* at http://www.bbc.co. uk/news/technology-18813237, http://www.bbc.co.uk/news/ technology-19093078 and http://www.bbc.co.uk/news/technology-19832043) is entirely irrelevant. What is clear is that through his Facebook page Hempfling is playing a magnificent role in helping people take the step towards a way of being with horses which is as potentially beneficial to the human as it is to the horse.

So how does Hempfling answer the question as to how to become the type of human a horse seeks to be with on his Facebook page or through his other communications, such as his books, articles and videos? One of Hempfling's most consistent answers to this question was provided again in his response to one of the comment posters on his Facebook page. In this particular case he likened the person who has not yet become the type of human a horse seeks to be with to an individual at the controls of a plane who has not yet learned to fly it. In the same way that a person needs to learn how to be a pilot before he flies a plane, so too should a human "Learn what you must learn before you are personally together with a horse, because you will actually be confronted with pretty much all the conceivable eventualities over time". And how and where should you learn this? The answer which Hempfling provides is this:

> Come to my school, and indeed for the longest possible time period if you really want to learn it – I don't know any better one and if you like my results, then confide in me. Now I'm advertising? Maybe so – but everything else would be hypocrisy! Too expensive? Think about what you in reality save and think about this: I give you in days or months, what I have spent a lifetime collecting, because all "instruction books" about the authentic being with horses are literally and in the true sense of the words burnt on the pyres of history.

The problems with this answer

There are a number of problems with this answer and the first has to do with the huge discrepancy between the dream which Hempfling presents, on the one hand, and what he actually offers and has managed to provide to date, on the other. The dream which Hempfling presents is epitomised in the video which he uses more than any other to market himself: that of himself and the Lipizzaner stallion, Ferdinand dancing at liberty, which by the time of writing had garnered an impressive 1,821,466 views. (You can watch it at http://www.youtube.com/watch?v=zq06bmJLt-U.) What Hempfling offers though are courses (largely without horses) which will not even come close to providing you with the qualities and tools that you will require if you are to achieve that dream. More importantly, by his own admission Hempfling has failed to pass on the ability to achieve that dream to any other human in more than twenty-odd years of teaching including his recent one-year course (which had a dropout rate of 30%).

There is another problem with this answer and it is this: it suggests that a person cannot or should not learn to be the kind of human a horse seeks to be with in the presence of a horse. Presumably, one must first spend a good deal of time learning and developing one's skills in a simulator like a trainee pilot, before one dares to go to one's horse. But as one of the participants in the debate on Hempfling's Facebook page asks, "How do we know when we are ready?" The answer to this question is easy: your horse will show you. Put another way, although you can work on your self-development in the absence of a horse, ultimately you can only learn to become the kind of human a horse seeks to be with in its presence. After all, it is your horse who will teach you, if you are open to what it tries to show you.

Revisiting the dream
At this point we may want to revisit the dream which Hempfling sells in his Ferdinand video commercial (the video was actually used as paid advertising on YouTube). The interaction that we see in the video is truly charming but we would do well to bear in mind that it is the product of extensive training and not just the relationship between horse and human. Hempfling had extensive sessions of training with Ferdinand on and off over a number of years before that video was filmed, and prior to that the horse had received conventional classical training with a bit in its mouth. It is also worth noting that Ferdinand is not Hempfling's horse.

The Hempfling Facebook page commentator with whom I have been corresponding is not so much inspired by Hempfling's dance with Ferdinand as by his relationship with his own horse, Janosch, the little chestnut gelding who features so prominently in *Dancing with Horses* (the book and the DVD, an excerpt of which can be viewed at http://www.youtube.com/watch?v=BVciE_KBLYg). This too is my inspiration. I would much rather have a relationship with a horse of my own which is as close as that between Hempfling and Janosch than the trained capability of dancing with a Ferdinand who belongs to someone else. It is clear that Janosch seeks the company and leadership of his human as part of a lasting relationship. So does Hempfling have any other answers to help us attain a similar relationship with our own horses?

Another of Hempfling's answers
There is another of Hempfling's answers to the question as to how to become the kind of human a horse seeks to be with which is absolutely spot on, and which reflects his true strength and largely explains his success in developing a relationship with those horses he allows us to see him with. This answer lies in developing spiritual and body awareness, so as to learn to be authentically yourself in the moment and to use your body effectively in the process. The underlying premise is that by being in the moment with your horse you will both be interacting with each other as authentic, sentient beings in the absence of all of the emotional and cognitive baggage that humans are wont to drag around with them, and that by using your body effectively, you will be able to communicate with your horse in a manner that engenders trust and understanding (that is, effective communication).

The spiritual aspect is not to be confused with religion, beliefs or mythology, although, like many other factors, these phenomena may have a bearing on one's spiritual development. Rather in this context "spiritual development" refers to the evolution of consciousness within the individual, where being fully conscious refers to the state of full awareness of one's being in the here and now, to the exclusion of the clutter of thought and emotion to which we humans almost constantly yield. To the extent that such consciousness also involves an awareness of one's physical being, it also covers body awareness. While body awareness extends beyond the spiritual, the development of both forms of awareness – spiritual and physical can go hand in hand through active meditation, such as the type practised by Hempfling through his body awareness exercises, archery and even – or perhaps especially – interaction with a horse.

In concrete terms

Of course, all of this is terribly abstract and, as such, frustratingly inaccessible, or so it seems. So let us reach for a concrete example as exhibited by someone who has shown himself to be extremely capable of moving into fully focused, intent-driven, coordinated awareness at the drop of a hat: Klaus Ferdinand Hempfling. Soon after the idea of this post first came to me while corresponding with the Hempfling's Facebook page commentator mentioned above, the man himself posted a video on YouTube, which features the very concrete awareness of which I speak. You can view it at http://www. youtube.com/watch?v=ijaET56K7Aw.

If you closely examine Hempfling in this brief video, you will notice the gracefully controlled energy of the human which is so typical of intent when it is packaged in highly focused, coordinated motion. Hempfling is entirely there in the very moment of being as it unfolds through his movement. This is consciousness: the full awareness of being. There is room for nothing else. And it is precisely and only in this state that the human is authentically who he is. The ability to be in this way is the flame that we are seeking to light, for it is precisely that which enables Hempfling to dance with Ferdinand in the open and which ultimately, if we extend it beyond our interaction with horses into our everyday life, can help us to live a happier and more fulfilling life. As Eckhart Tolle puts it:

> When you are present, when your attention is fully and intensely in the Now, Being can be felt but it can never be understood mentally. To regain awareness of Being and to abide in that state of "feeling-realisation" is enlightenment.
>
> (*The Power of Now*, p. 13)

So where do I start?

Quite frankly, I have only a vague idea of where you should start. In fact, you are the only one who knows exactly where you do. You start precisely where you are, and the nature of your situation is something which you know better than anyone else. All it takes really is a desire to start: a commitment. This is the first step and perhaps both the easiest and the toughest to take. It is easy because you have the desire but it is tough, because it requires a bit of self-discipline. From there on in it is simply a matter of looking around you for practical ways of living that commitment.

I hear you groan. That is where the rub is, isn't it? What exactly are those practical ways. Should you attend a lengthy Hempfling course or courses (the short courses will only allow you to sniff at the possibilities), assuming you can afford his over-inflated prices or are willing to sell your car or indebt yourself to your family (or whatever) to make the kind of sacrifice that a committed disciple will readily undertake for his acknowledged master? And if you do, will you really be the first to come away with the expertise and composure that will enable you to dance with your horse the way Hempfling does with Ferdinand and no one else ever has? Or is there another way?

Another way
Vicki attended three courses with Hempfling in Denmark, had a great time doing so and learned a fair amount that has helped her on her journey. I, on the other hand, may be one of the most motivated students of Hempfling who has never attended any of his courses. Fortunately, I have had the opportunity to learn from numerous people who have spent time studying or working with Hempfling, including former students, assistants and his most senior body awareness coach at the time.

This has helped me acquire enough knowledge and experience to help me look for and find another way. As I have gone about this, I have recorded some of my experiences in this blog. While participating in the debate on Hempfling's Facebook page my correspondent had their attention drawn by someone else to this blog and started to read it. I am aware that trawling this blog for clues as to how I found another way requires a good deal of reading. My correspondent is undaunted. It is my hope that others will also find clues to another way in these pages. I would not presume to dictate another way for you to travel. Only you can do that. What I can do, is simply share some of my experiences with you as I have done in this blog but perhaps I can make it easier by condensing them into fewer pages and sharing them with you in a more readily digestible form. This I hope to do over the next few months. Let us see how we go.

Noora Ehnqvist, and Body and Spiritual Awareness
8 July 2013

Last month Vicki and I attended the first two days of a three-day horse and human clinic given in the Netherlands by Noora Ehnqvist, a young Finnish horsewoman and former student of and assistant to Klaus Ferdinand Hempfling, who has taken what she has learned from the master who dances with horses and others to create her own unique approach towards helping people become the kind of human whom a horse seeks to be with. It was an experience which made a huge impression on me and which has since helped me to take my relationship with my mare, Pip, to the next level, not due to any new insight that I may have gained into horses but because it helped me to put familiar theory into everyday practice.

The ideas
The course, which was hosted by Marijke de Jong of classical riding straightness training fame, with whom Noora Ehnqvist has teamed up to learn from each other and help others on the journey with horses, was open to everyone on the first day and about seventy people (of whom only two were male) availed themselves of the opportunity to attend. Noora spent the morning introducing us to the ideas behind her approach, which she stressed was not a theory, philosophy or method but was simply based on universal wisdom.

Essentially, what we humans should be seeking to achieve with or without horses is presence: being accompanied by the awareness of being in the very moment of being. To achieve this, according to Noora, we need to relearn how to be when we move and when we are motionless, to become centred or grounded. This refers to the ability to direct your presence from your core, finding joy, softness and inner peace coupled with spirit, energy and clarity. This entails that we humans need to find within ourselves the ability to be empathetic and empowering in our dealings with others, including our horses. "For horses pressure is an enormous thing," says Noora. "Horses do not have a voice to express pain!" We need to move away from bossing our horses around to finding within them a willing partner.

Putting these ideas into practice occurred in two main ways during the clinic. First, there were sessions involving humans and horses selected from amongst the advanced students of Marijke de Jong and her assistant, Claudia Wolters. A number of these students are in turn straightness training instructors, so the lessons which they learned during the Noora Ehnqvist clinic have the potential to reach others who were not fortunate enough to attend it.

The first day
On the first day we watched two humans interact with their horses under Noora's guidance. First there was Lucie and her seven-year-old Andalusian stallion, Senillius. Born in Spain and sold to Germany and then the Netherlands, this young horse was quiet and dull with low energy levels. The stallion was not helped much by his owner, as she seemed to move mechanically with her horse. Noora took over and showed us how to move from the core, to reinvigorate the horse through softness coupled with joyful energy and clarity. Senillius lit up and began to move with greater vigour. The session ended on a high for him and for his owner.

Judith and her two-and-a-half-year-old Dutch pony, Angel, were next. Angel was clearly nervous and anxious first with her owner and then with Noora. Alone with Angel in the picadero (a relatively small, square exercise area), Noora deliberately avoided seeking contact with the pony, as she calmly walked around aware of what both she and Angel were doing. Bit by bit the pony began to seek contact, coming in towards Noora, moving away and then coming in even closer until horse and human were walking calmly together. Judith then took over, holding Angel on a long lead. Unfortunately, she was too busy and her unrestrained movements caused her horse to respond accordingly. The calm disappeared. Noora pointed this out to Judith and showed her how to move and use the lead to find a calm, willing partner in her pony. With Noora's guidance and encouragement Judith started moving with greater presence and Angel responded. By the end of the session horse and human were calmly working and walking together. Everyone was impressed.

Practice: body awareness

The second way in which Noora Ehnqvist's ideas were put into practice took the form of body awareness exercises interspersed between the main sessions. Noora demonstrated the difference between unaware movement and motion guided by awareness and directed from the core starting from the basics: how you stand, how you walk and how you run. There are mindless, tiring ways of standing, walking and running. Most people employ them. There is also a conscious way of doing the same thing, one involving an awareness of ourselves and our surroundings, consciously directing our movement from our core.

Noora also introduced other body awareness exercises but more as a demonstration of the possibilities than as a training session, because the group was too large to permit much more. Neither did the weather help, as the skies broke and the rain drove us indoors. Nevertheless, enough seemed to have been achieved to help some of the advanced students in the interaction with their horses the next day.

Empowered

The rest of the Noora Ehnqvist clinic was confined to the advanced students of Marijke de Jong and Claudia Wolters but for some reason Vicki and I were invited back, giving us a total of about 35 participants on the second day. We would have liked to attend the entire clinic but we had taken on too much work to permit that. The day started off with a vivid example of what can happen, if a human lacks presence. A Belgian instructor and her eight-year-old PRE gelding, Offendido, entered the picadero. The horse was lifeless, going through the motions like a robot in response to his owner, who adopted a businesslike approach, making him move as and when she required. No amount of guidance from Noora seemed to help the human adopt a different approach. It was interesting to note that the Belgian instructor had been absent from the body awareness sessions.

In the course of the day we viewed a number of humans interacting with their horses and in all but one case I noted how the connection between horse and human improved, once the human became more centred and started to move more consciously. Two of the highlights were the sessions with the two humans whom we had seen the day before. Judith returned with Angel and it was clear to everyone that the human was far more grounded and aware than she had been the day before, and the pony responded accordingly. Lucie was back as well but this time with Bombero (stable name: Beer), a seven-year-old PRE gelding born in Spain who has a health issue in his right leg causing him to walk short and to object to training. It was refreshing to see how differently Lucie was moving: not as casual as the day before but calmer, more aware and with greater clarity. Under Noora's guidance she learned to observe her horse closely and respond to it more readily. Coupled with the close connection which she had clearly developed with her horse, this helped Lucy to bring Beer to the stage where he could cope with and actually enjoy the training. Both women had clearly been empowered through Noora Ehnqvist's assistance.

Unfair comparisons
Vicki knows Noora Ehnqvist from the three courses she attended with Klaus Ferdinand Hempfling in 2010. By that stage Noora had spent several years learning from Hempfling on and off first as a student and later as an assistant, in which capacity she also taught body awareness to Hempfling's students from around the world under his auspices, including Vicki. At no stage, however, was she granted accreditation as a Hempfling body awareness instructor, because she did not attend the formal, expensive courses required for that purpose.

It was therefore inevitable that we would be looking for the Hempfling influences and be tempted to make unfair comparisons. According to Vicki, the Hempfling influences are definitely there but, as I see it, Noora has taken what she has learned from him and others and is using it to empower humans and through them, their horses. Unlike Hempfling, she does not get to choose which horses and humans she is going to help. This is not about people coming to watch Noora Ehnqvist in action with horses. She takes the horses and humans as they come and she helps them to help each other.

Lessons learned

If there are any lessons which I learned during the Noora Ehnqvist clinic, those that I am particularly conscious of are these. First of all, I realised that in my dealings with Pip, especially when it comes to training, I am so tempted to get it right, that I sometimes end up making her do things. At the end of the day, everyone can make a horse move in a certain way. Some of us just learn to do it with greater ease and dexterity. The challenge though is not to make my mare move but to encourage her to want to do so. Pip must be a willing partner. Anything less is unacceptable. This is something that I have been aware of in theory for some time. Putting it into practice since the clinic has been beneficial to both Pip and myself. Thank you, Noora Ehnqvist.

In the time that I spent learning Hempfling's body awareness exercises in the past and have spent doing Tai Chi since that avenue was effectively closed to me, I have become aware of the need to learn to be, to be aware of being, and to act from my core while doing so. Of course, the challenge lies in extending this awareness beyond my Tai Chi sessions into my everyday life and, in particular, my interaction with horses. While I have been aware of this in theory, it was good to have this driven home again in practice. Thank you, Noora Ehnqvist.

Body and spiritual awareness

Reporting on the Noora Ehnqvist clinic seems to be an appropriate follow-on to my last post discussing where humans can start with horses. Ultimately, as Noora shows, we start with ourselves, which is not to suggest that we need to leave our horses and enter a wallet-blowout, three-month retreat with some or other dream-selling guru, before we are ready to face our equine friends. Rather, it is to propose that a change needs to occur within ourselves, if we are to find willing partners in our horses, a change that can occur while we interact with our horses on a regular basis.

This change can be initiated by embarking on a process of body and spiritual awareness. The two go hand-in-hand, if only because the spiritual awareness I am referring to is not some pie-in-the-sky affair but a very real consciousness of being in the very moment of being, what Eckhart Tolle calls "the power of now". And this spiritual power is intimately connected with our awareness of our body and our surroundings in the moment of now. So how can you achieve this?

> Being is not only beyond but also deep within every form as its innermost invisible and indestructible essence. This means that it is accessible to you now as our own deepest self, your true nature. But don't seek to grasp it with your mind. Don't try to understand it.
>
> You can only know it when the mind is still. When you are present, when your attention is fully and intensely in the Now, Being can be felt but it can never be understood mentally.
>
> To regain awareness of Being and to abide in that state of "feeling realisation" is enlightenment.
>
> Eckhart Tolle, *Practising the Power of Now*, p. 8

Grounding: the position

Actually, it is pretty simple if not always easy to achieve. Let me illustrate this. There is a starting position for physical activity in a number of Asian martial arts traditions, which Hempfling has included as part of his approach to body awareness and which I first learned from Vicki following her return from the Hempfling courses that she attended in 2010, and later from Hempfling's senior body awareness coach, Jo Ross. It is called the ground position in Hempfling-speak and is the starting point for all body awareness exercises in that it helps to ground or centre the human.

Essentially, you stand up straight, ensure that your knees are not locked, spread your legs until your feet are roughly in line with your shoulders, relax your entire upper body, and tilt your pelvis forward and up. If you do this properly, you should have the feeling that you are circling your pelvis upwards and that you are sitting on your hips and upper thighs, as it were. Should this be your first attempt, you may also feel that you are leaning too far forward. Actually, if you look at yourself sideways in the mirror, you will probably notice that your back is straighter than it has ever been and that you are not leaning backwards, as most people do when they believe that they are standing up straight. You may also notice that your posture in this position closely resembles what it would be if you were sitting astride a horse.

Grounding: the awareness

Now, while you are holding the ground position, focus on your breathing. What we are aiming for is to learn to breathe from our core, the space within your abdomen. When you inhale, you should have the feeling that you are drawing in air down to your core without undue effort or expanding your body. And when you exhale, you should have the feeling that you are drawing the air from your core as your abdomen expands slightly. If you put effort into this exhalation as you will do when performing body awareness exercises, you will find that it is a source of power and balance.

As you stand in the ground position breathing from the core, focus your attention on your head. How does it feel? How do you feel about it? Then move to your neck and do likewise. Repeat this then for the various parts of your body as you move gradually your attention down to your feet. By then you should have a close awareness of your body and your core, from which all movement will now emanate. Hold on to that awareness, as you now shift your attention to your surroundings. What do you hear? What do you see? What do you smell? Can you feel the air on your skin? Can you taste it? Focus closely on what you experience within and without you. By this stage you will have no capacity to entertain thought, as every part of you will be concentrated on the here and now. How do you feel? Alive? In body and spirit? Welcome to the power of now. You are grounded. You are, and you are aware that you are. This is it: this is being and the awareness of being ... in the moment.

Grounding: going into the moment

The grounding (some prefer to call it "centring") process that I describe here is a very powerful path towards banishing anxiety, self-doubt or any other thought or emotion which has the capacity to sap your strength and dissipate your power. It can also serve as an incredibly useful one or two-minute preparation interval prior to interacting with your horse. Try it just before you go to your equine friend and you will probably notice that by the time the two of you are together, there is nothing other than horse and human, and the surroundings through which the two of you are moving together, which may or may not include other humans and/or horses. You will be as in the moment as your horse.

Of course, you need not confine grounding to the times that you spend with your horse. I have found it useful to incorporate various aspects in my everyday life. You can start with little things. For instance, one of the first things I tried to do was to ensure that I was fully aware of all that I was experiencing within and without me while washing my face and brushing my teeth in the morning. It is not easy. In fact, it is astounding to consciously note how your mind insists on taking over your life, as thoughts and emotions muscle their way in. I am now trying to adopt a similar approach with other mundane activities, such as doing the washing up, clearing weeds in the garden and so forth.

It is also possible to focus on bigger picture activities. One of the first things that I focused on was to learn how to stand upright without locking my knees. You become very conscious of how you are standing if you try this. It took about a year before I started automatically standing with my knees unlocked and hence ever so slightly bent, with the result that I now have greater and more conscious control over my body and balance. What I am now working on is learning to breathe and move automatically from my core, not just when I am with my horse or doing body awareness exercises but always. This is a huge challenge but I find that I am more conscious of how I am breathing and moving with greater frequency throughout the day.

Tai Chi

One of the main problems with the body awareness regimes offered by people such as Klaus Ferdinand Hempfling and Noora Ehnqvist is that you can learn how to do the exercises during their courses but everything eventually falls apart following your return home, because no instructors are readily available, nor is there any reference to consult in order to ensure that you are doing those exercises properly. In the past Hempfling accredited a number of body awareness instructors who had attended very expensive initial and refresher body awareness courses, and placed their names on his website. However, those names disappeared when he updated his website recently. Hempfling also informed his remaining one-year school students that they had qualified as body awareness mentors. However, their names have never appeared on his website. In addition, neither Hempfling nor Ehnqvist have books or videos available to serve as a reference and their courses are not readily available to the vast majority of people for one reason or another.

By way of a replacement for those body awareness exercises I have opted for Tai Chi, because of its widespread availability in the form of courses, books and/or videos. Personally, I would prefer the body awareness exercises offered by Hempfling and Ehnqvist, so this is a compromise as far as I am concerned. In particular, I have opted for Dr Yang Jwing-Ming's *Tai Chi Chuan: Classical Yang Style* (available in the form of a book and accompanying DVD), because it is a "slow and relaxed moving meditation" (p. 1) and arguably comes closest to the approach embodied in Hempfling's and Ehnqvist's body awareness exercises. It also includes Qigong and detailed explanations of breathing techniques and the history and philosophy underlying taijiquan (an alternative spelling to tai chi chuan).

I have found it particularly beneficial to start the day with the Qigong warm-up exercises and the eight fundamental stances preceded by an introductory grounding, as described above. In between the various exercises and stances I return to the ground position and throughout it all I focus on my breathing and movement from my core. It is then possible to add various other Tai Chi movements as one goes. Ultimately, what it is about is nurturing a new approach to life through active meditation rather than slavishly following a particular form of Tai Chi.

Corroboree Equus, Our Horses and Hempfling Students
16 August 2013

Here in the Netherlands we have been enjoying the most amazing summer with temperatures well into the twenties and even the lower thirties, making up for a long cold winter with snow on the ground way past when we would normally expect it. The silly season is upon us, which means that we have a bit more time to spend with our horses and to plan. It also seems to be an appropriate time to fill you in on the Corroboree Equus, our latest plans, how our horses are faring and unexpected developments on the Hempfling front.

Trip to Australia and New Zealand
It has been well over two years since Vicki and I left Australia for Europe with our mare, Anaïs, and our dog, Dubu, for the purposes of attending Klaus Ferdinand Hempfling's one-year schooling course. We left behind two retired geldings, Gulliver and Farinelli, who are being professionally looked after for us on a magnificent property in south-east Queensland. We feel that it is time for us to return to Australia and see for ourselves how they are faring and to visit our friends around the country and in New Zealand at the same time. We will be spending a month visiting both countries from the last week of September.

Here in Europe what passes for our leaders are hell-bent on sending huge swathes of ordinary people back into Third World conditions, especially in southern Europe, as they seek to make them pay for the past mistakes of big business and corrupt politicians, and to make European multinationals more competitive with the emerging economies of Asia, Africa and Latin America. As a result Europe is locked in a deepening recession in most parts of the

60

continent, which is having a major impact on entire industries, including ours (translation). We are currently facing the challenge of reinventing ourselves and our trip to Australia will help us to decide whether that should occur there or here in Europe.

Corroboree Equus
The inaugural Corroboree Equus will be held in Tallangatta, Victoria, Australia. If you are committed to a new way of being with horses, one in which the horse is invited to be a willing partner rather than merely an instrument for the achievement of a human's equestrian aspirations or an accessory to a human ego, you are welcome to join many others like yourself to share experiences, learn from each other and have fun together. If you're expecting to be hit with an attendance fee, relax. There is none. Yep, it's absolutely free of charge.

Vicki and I will be attending the Corroboree Equus and look forward to meeting any of our readers who will be there. If you choose to bring your horse along, we look forward to meeting your equine friend as well. By all accounts it promises to be a great event in a relaxed environment within a beautiful part of the country. So if you can make it, we look forward to getting together with you and other like-minded spirits.

A new equine home
In my post of 14 May (*Our Horses Banished by the Ice Queen*) I mentioned that our horses had been thrown out of their former livery yard and that we had found temporary accommodation for them elsewhere. For several weeks they shared a paddock and two stables on a property in the process of being sold not too far from where we live. It was good to be responsible for every aspect of our horses' well-being again. Unfortunately, it was not sustainable for a number of reasons, our travels being one of them.

Fortunately, we managed to find permanent accommodation for Anaïs and Pip, when two places became available at a livery yard about a twelve-minute drive from where we live. Again we were lucky to find a facility within a few hundred metres of one of the most beautiful forests I have ever had the good fortune to walk in here in the Netherlands. Unfortunately, there is downside to the warmer temperatures of summer in the form of swarms of horse flies which render it almost impossible to do much outside with our horses, let alone go for walks in the forest with them. It is actually so bad that the horses have to be stabled during the day and spend the nights out in the field. Fortunately, there is an upside to this. The stables are cool during the heat of the day and the nights are free of horse flies.

Body balancing with Pip

Pip and I are making visible progress with our body balancing exercises. I am finding that my daily Tai Chi sessions are helping me to move and breathe in a more balanced and grounded way not only during those sessions but in everyday activities, especially together with my mare. Nevertheless, there are still moments when I hang my head in shame, realising that I have been focusing so intently on completing an exercise properly, that I have ignored, if not hurt, the feelings of my equine friend. The boss mentality, I find, is so difficult to shake. Admittedly though, I am encountering this difficulty far less frequently than in the past.

And there is no reason for it either, because Pip is doing so well. She is carrying herself better and is far more balanced in her movement. Whereas she used to drag her inside right in the past, she is now beginning to step under. The change in her balance is also slowly starting to be reflected in her feet. I am beginning to notice that her right fore hoof is gradually displaying more concavity, although I feel that the overall change is going to require a good deal of time. In addition, the small hard muscles which she used to have in her neck and shoulders have become softer and longer, which means that she is finding it easier to flex.

Collection and riding

In fact, Pip is doing so well that I am now seriously starting to prepare her for riding. Vicki has been on her back on about four occasions now using a bareback pad, the first time that Pip has had anyone on her back in fifteen months. For the moment we have simply been checking to see how Pip responds, getting her used to the feeling again, and helping her to learn a new way of carrying a human in the absence of a bit or any force by reproducing what we are doing on the ground on her back. Yesterday was major. You should have seen how she and Vicki were communicating with each other without a bit, without a saddle, and without any force whatsoever. Pip had a few minor misgivings in the beginning but now that she realises that force is no longer involved, she is beginning to relax and gain more confidence.

Now I am beginning to focus on teaching Pip how to collect herself on the ground. I am using a cordeo as a tool to ask her to lift the base of her neck without raising her head. Once this is established, I am hoping to help her bring her hind feet further under her. This should have the effect of shifting more of her weight to her hindquarters, which should theoretically make it easier for her to carry a rider. In addition, I am continuing to help Pip strengthen her abdominal muscles and hindquarters with various exercises. This should make it easier to achieve this shift in weight.

Talking to the animals

If you have ever felt that I am losing the plot, as one former friend has, here is a chance for you to gather evidence to the effect that this has really occurred. I talk to the animals. But wait, there is more: they are responding to it. The first time I noticed it was a good few months ago when I was lungeing Anaïs over some cavalletti. On the right she was fine but on the left she was hesitant. So I spoke to her and told her that she could ignore the cavalletti if she wanted to and just pass in front of it but, if she felt confident enough, she could go ahead and do it. She took me at my word, passed on the inner side twice and then, without me asking for it, moved out and took the cavalletti on the third pass.

Although I was quite amazed at the time, I let it pass and did not pursue a similar approach with Pip. Until a few weeks ago, that is, when while waiting for Vicki and Anaïs to finish their lesson, I started scratching Pip and asked her to move her body, so that my hand was over the areas that she wanted me to address. She did. Her lower neck and shoulders on both sides: get busy, Andrew, so I did. she loved it, raising her head and pressing her muzzle into a point extruding over her lower lip. Now we start off every session with scratching and she is a different horse as a result. Not content to let a good thing slide, I decided to start explaining each exercise to Pip before we tried it. Shoulder-in at the trot was a prime example. I used my hand to show her the shape we were aiming for, explained how we might want to try it, and mentioned that it could have major benefits for her physical and mental well-being. What does Pip do now? She actually starts to initiate some of the action. Yesterday, for instance, she decided that it was time to trot and pick up some speed before moving into shoulder-in, so yours truly found himself trying to keep up with his horse. So much for being the great leader.

Message from Hempfling students

Some of you may have read a message sent to our readers and ourselves in the form of a comment by Nanda and Karina, two of the seven students (originally ten) remaining in Hempfling's one-year school. If you have not, here it is:

> Dear Andrew and readers,
>
> We, Nanda and Karina, would like to reply to your post and give you a short insight in our experience of the one-year-schooling and of Klaus, as a teacher and as a person.
>
> For us, the aim is to become authentic beings and find our own purpose in life. For some this could mean to be the best coach, teacher or manager, for others it could mean to be with horses in their authentic way, or just to be the best mother.

This is what Klaus offers, tools and true insights in yourself, but you have to be open to receive this. From there on, it has to be your work and your path to follow. Klaus has given us exactly that. He is a great teacher and coach and is that person that he is showing with the horses.

After 11 months (10 months last year and 1 month in March), we are finishing this summer with 6 more weeks, the one-year-schooling. Some of us are doing parts of the remaining course with family. We are following our paths...

Best regards

It appears that after close to two years Hempfling's first full one-year schooling course is finally drawing to a close with possibly as many as seven of the ten students who originally started out at the beginning of September 2011. Amongst other things, they conclude that Hempfling is "great teacher and coach and is that person that he is showing with the horses".

Which leads me to ask: which horses? Jo's stallion, Habanero, which Hempfling effectively took over instead of helping his student become the horse's friend and leader? Jasmijn's three stallions, with whom she was dancing before she attended the one-year school and with whom she has danced as well since leaving his school prematurely (see my post entitled *Hempfling's Student: Casting off the Master's Shadow?*)? And what of Karina's horses, in particular, Cody (see my post entitled *Breaking the Cycle of Chaos* in *In Search of the Master Who Dances with Horses:Challenge*)? I invited Nanda and Karina to share their experiences of the one year school with us by publishing their separate stories on our blog on condition that we could present them with questions about those experiences. Their reply has taken the form of a lengthy silence.

I, in particular, would have loved to have heard from Nanda how it was possible that she, an experienced horse person, could have grown to be afraid of little Cody. I would also have liked to have asked Karina, Cody's owner, why she allowed him to be condemned to his fate in the presence of the great horse lover, Hempfling, and his one-year students. I would also have liked to have asked them why there was such a high drop-out rate (30%) for a course that was so expensive (EUR 84,000.00). In fact, I would have liked to have asked whether all of the disturbing things that I have personally heard from some of their fellow students is true or just the product of a nightmare.

The master at work

Which is not to deny that Hempfling is doing great work in helping people from around the world find a new way of being with horses. In fact I would urge you to have a look at his Facebook page. What is exciting about what Hempfling is doing now is that he is actually working increasingly with ordinary horses (even mares, which represents a major breakthrough) and not just the ones that look good on video (for instance, horses with a Baroque frame, such as the conventionally trained Lipizzaner stallion, Ferdinand, and the Spanish PRE stallion, Habanero), that he is riding them and not just talking about it, and that he is doing all of this without using instruments of force. It is also good to see that Hempfling's new centre has decent fencing for the horses, and to read that its new bistro is serving organic food.

Becoming the Kind of Human a Horse Seeks to be With: Part 1

14 September 2013

As we move into the latter half of September, I am acutely conscious of a convergence of developments which are inviting me to contemplate what is required of the human, if the latter is to become someone whom a horse wishes to be with. Not only does this question penetrate to the core of my relationship with Pip, it is also the subject of a presentation which I will be giving in Australia later this month. As I prepare for it, I find myself drawing inspiration again from a man who is currently guiding the remnants of his one-year school students through the final stages of a course which is devoted in part to this very issue.

Corroboree Equus

Vicki and I have just returned from a visit to her twin sister, Agathe, and her partner, Ron, in Malaga, Spain, a dress rehearsal for our trip to Australia next week. While in Australia we will be attending the inaugural Corroboree Equus, where we will both be giving presentations which essentially deal with the horse's choice as to whether or not to interact with a human and what the latter is called upon to do, if the horse is to be a willing partner in this process.

Our preparations are acting as a springboard for the most animated debates concerning the various guides who have inspired us. Does Nevzorov really offer a horse a free choice when he separates it from its kind to train it in isolation within a relatively confined space that is screened off from the outside world by high, largely windowless (to all intents and purposes) walls and a roof? Are not some of Carolyn Resnick's waterhole rituals based on negative reinforcement? Is Hempfling's control over a horse's movement not much better? Can Mark Rashid and Frédéric Pignon really offer a horse freedom of choice with a bit in its mouth? Does Chuck Mintzlaff's friendship training not try and condition a horse through the use of food? Imke Spilker may indeed befriend her horse as an equal partner but is she not fooling yourself by refusing to acknowledge her dominant status as a guide and protector? And what of Michael Bevilacqua? How did he come to horses so late and yet manage to be friend, protector and guide to his horses in a herd under the wide open skies?

My presentation

Perhaps you will indulge me if I set out the approach which I have adopted in my preliminary draft and ask you to shoot holes in it. I start by examining the meaning of the statement, *becoming the kind of human horse seeks to be with*. Does it not imply freedom of choice on the part of the horse? After all, does it not suggest that the horse may choose to be with a human or not? Does it not also imply that, unless the human is intuitively present and aware, they will need to change in order to become someone whom the horse seeks to be with?

So what is required in order to become such a human? Perhaps there are certain things which a horse enjoys and which you can do with it as a friend. Perhaps there are also other things that you can provide to a horse as its protector and guide, such as care and training. Yet are there not also qualities which a human requires, if those other things are not to fall short? And if there are, what are they?

Bevilacqua and Hempfling

I look for examples of those qualities in the inspirational books, videos and other materials at my disposal and keep coming back to two people: Michael Bevilacqua and Klaus Ferdinand Hempfling. Such qualities seem to have developed naturally within Michael Bevilacqua, while in Hempfling's case there seems to be a constant battle between the man who he is and the human whom he wishes to become. To this extent I find myself identifying more readily with Hempfling than with Bevilacqua, for it is a struggle that I too have had to contend with every single day.

In Hempfling I find the focus where I need it to be: on the human rather than on the horse. This is not to say that Hempfling offers us examples of the qualities that we need to have, if a horse is to seek to be with us, and that Bevilacqua does not. On the contrary, those qualities are more readily apparent in Bevilacqua and seemed to come more naturally to him. Hempfling, on the other hand, has had to devise ways to acquire those qualities and he is prepared to exhibit them to whomever has the desire and money to acquire them through his books, videos, courses and body awareness coaches. The upshot is that Hempfling will be featuring rather prominently in my presentation at the Corroboree Equus.

The KFH one-year school

Some two years after it began, what remains of Hempfling's first full-time, one-year school is limping to an end on the back of the master's Summer Academy. Gone is his undertaking that no more than ten students would be taught at a time. Gone is the accommodation that his students were promised. Gone is the commitment to allow his students to qualify as horse practitioners in addition to body awareness coaches. Gone are 30% of the students who started the course. Gone are 70% of the horses that started it with them. And gone is any form of critical questioning of the master on the part of his remaining one-year students which could in any way be interpreted as a sign of leadership and a refusal to indulge in servile hero-worship.

Yet there is a silver lining to this sorry story, as there is too of many of the clouds that initially appeared to be so big and black. The last two courses available to the one-year students as part of Hempfling's summer academy are designed to provide skills and qualifications to those interested in qualifying as a KFH body awareness coach for general and horse-related purposes. Of course, the distinction is absurd, because it is my experience that

Hempfling's general body awareness exercises can play a key role in helping anyone to become a human with whom a horse seeks to be with, whether they are specifically geared to horses or not. And it is precisely in this area – and not in relation to the training of horses – that Hempfling's skills as an educator lie. As he himself once mentioned to me during a telephone call while preparing to host a body awareness course under the guidance of his then sole senior body awareness coach, Jo Ross, in March 2011, "I train people, not horses".

Challenges and opportunities
Some of Hempfling's one-year students may be seen in one of his recent YouTube videos, a number of them familiar faces from the past. It is sobering to realise that Vicki and I came so close to studying with them. They will be completing their course with hopefully at least one of the two KFH body awareness qualifications that are also being offered to anyone else who may be interested in paying the roughly EUR 12,000.00 required to attend them after completing a few weeks of qualifying study by way of a prerequisite, as opposed to the full year of study which the one-year students will have completed over two years and for which a fee of EUR 84,000.00 was charged. While it may not seem fair, such a qualification would at least provide the one-year students with the means to start earning an income as KFH body awareness coaches.

Of course, the one-year students will also have to contend with challenges. The course fee of EUR 84,000.00 represents a major investment, which has been compounded by food costs and significantly more extensive travel expenses as a result of unscheduled study intervals due to poor course planning (the course had to be interrupted a number of times to deal with the visa issues faced by those one-year students from outside the EU). Based on Hempfling's previous body awareness instructor regime they are also likely to be required to attend expensive refresher courses at regular intervals, if they wish to remain qualified. A great deal of work will be required of the one-year students if they are to recoup their investment.

More challenges and best wishes
In addition, those students who qualify as KFH body awareness coaches at the end of this month will have to compete with people such as Noora Ehnqvist and Jasmijn Wauters, who can rightfully claim in their publicity materials that they have studied body awareness intensively with Hempfling over a considerable period of time. They will also have to compete with instructors who offer Feldenkrais and Tai Chi (two of the disciplines from which Hempfling has drawn heavily upon in the development of his body awareness system). Tai Chi courses are widely available and the costs involved are considerably less than the EUR 250.00 which I have seen charged for a two-day KFH body awareness course. In addition, no course materials are available for students to take home with them, so as to enable them to continue the body awareness exercises at home, whereas numerous Feldenkrais and Tai Chi books and videos are readily available, some even free of charge on YouTube.

In the face of these significant challenges I would like to wish Jo, Kate, Karina, Nanda and the other remaining one-year students the very best for the future. May you find fulfilment in helping others become the kind of human a horse seeks to be with.

Freedom for a former dressage performer
Following our return from Spain it occurred to me that not only had Vicki and I enjoyed a very special time with Agathe and Ron, but we had also witnessed something truly beautiful. Four months ago Agathe had left the Netherlands with her 17-year-old warmblood mare, Ochet, to start a new life in Spain. This move has been major for both horse and human but perhaps even more for the horse. Born and bred in the Netherlands, Ochet had been trained to do dressage and had been ridden in competitions around this cool-climate country for her much of her life. Her move to Spain has marked her

retirement from the sport and the start of a life of unprecedented freedom.

Ochet has traded in her small stable in a livery yard accommodating some 280 horses close to Amsterdam's Schiphol Airport for a seemingly endless, unfenced hillside across which she runs with a herd of other lucky horses. Yes, she has lost weight. Yes, she still has to acclimatise. And yes, she nurses minor cuts and bruises from time to time. Yet she is fit, her coat is glowing and her eyes are bright. This is a horse that is revelling in her freedom and her owner is happy to see her do so. This leaves a tiny fraction of just under half a million horses remaining to be liberated in the Netherlands.

The paradox that is Andalucía

Though brief, our stay in Spain was also very special for another reason. As we will be doing during our trip to Australia in ten days' time, we have been exploring the possibility of a move to Andalucía to join Agathe and Ron. To do so would be a challenge, as the region is rather undeveloped in relation to aspects which we feel are so important, such as the availability of organic and vegetarian foods, and holistic health care for ourselves and our horses.

Yet Andalucía also offers something which the Netherlands has largely lost: the capacity to enjoy life at an unhurried, spontaneous pace in spite of the huge socio-economic challenges which the area currently faces. Apart from being dirt cheap to live, work and play, it is also a region which has much to offer in the way of both everyday and high-brow culture, from the imposing structures of the Romans, Moors and Christians through to flamenco, Lorca, Picasso, *pueblos blancas* and excellent, affordable wines. And not to forget, it is the birthplace and home to one of the noblest breeds of horses, the Andalusian and its Carthusian variant (*Cartujano*). Andalucía is where Jo's stallion, Habanero (which features so prominently in many of Hempfling's recent videos) comes from, as do Jasmijn's former stallion, Esperado, and her current one, Eno del Cid.

The qualities

But I digress. So what are these qualities that a human requires if they wish to become someone whom a horse seeks to be with. Based on my study of Hempfling's teachings as expressed in his books and videos, articles with or about him, and written and verbal accounts given by numerous students who have attended his one-year and other courses, I have come up with the following list:

- contentment, relaxation and inner strength;
- trustworthiness and reliability;
- intent, clarity and the ability to communicate;
- a capacity for empathy and empowerment;
- authenticity and intuition: presence in the moment.

As I read this list, it occurs to me that, if these are the qualities one requires to become a human whom horses seek to be with and one was to actually acquire them, one would become a vastly better human being in the process. To this extent it seems to me that the journey towards becoming a human whom horses seek to be with represents an opportunity to reclaim our humanity, to turn our back on all that which insists on commoditising life and reducing it to transactions of profit and loss, and to claim instead the freedom to be, which is our birthright.

Reclaiming our humanity

So how can we acquire the qualities that I have mentioned and reclaim our humanity? This is a question that I am currently considering as I prepare for my presentation at the Corroboree Equus. I hope to offer a few ideas in my next post, which I would like to publish while in Australia.

Reply to Hempfling's One-year Students

26 September 2013

During the evening of Sunday, 15 September, Klaus Ferdinand Hempfling's remaining seven one-year students sent me a public letter through the comments section of this blog. It is a letter which challenges some of the most fundamental principles and values which I have come to espouse through some of the developments that I have recorded in this blog. It is also a letter that is highly critical of some of the statements which I have made in this blog. Accordingly, I am replying to this letter in the form of a special post on this blog.

Hempfling's one-year students' letter

Letter for Andrew

It's always easy not to live your own life but instead to criticize the massive and therefore publicly exposed life of someone else. We have personally experienced KFH for at least two years and we can all only say about your blog, that nothing of this has anything to do with the reality of this man and his teachings.

This man will certainly be mentioned in history, because of the things he has accomplished through his own massively hard work and in spite of resistance from people like you.

It would show good character, if you would at least keep your hands off everything he is doing. But instead it seems you take all you can get out of him and his accomplishments for free, just as you please, and in the same breath you write one negative thing after the other.

One thing still needs to be said: what if you, at the end of your life conclude, that you were simply mistaken? That you have spent so much time and so much effort in your life doing everything possible to really hurt one of the greatest horse

74

people and philosophers in every way you could. What then? Where then is your own time and your own life?

Your words emanate for us only one single desire: only once to be like this man whom you are disgusted by so much. Just once, one single time to be so great, so honest, so authentic, so strong, so caring, so joyful and so respected.

Inner and outer beauty has always stood in contrast to the people who are not able to accomplish anything on their own, which define themselves only by trying with all means to destroy what other people accomplished.

Isn't it so that you once wanted something from Klaus but didn't get it in the way that you thought? As well known, the fruits, which are hanging too high, do in our imagination quickly get very sour. Even if it does not happen now – Time will enlighten dark activities.

It's never too late to take on better ideas and it's never too late to admit a mistake and to turn towards life anew.

Stop with your public guessing about Klaus, the School and us.

Stop writing about Klaus, the School and us.

KFH One-Year-School students: Vera, Nanda, Karina, Cecile, Kate, Klaudia and Jo

My reply

Dear Vera, Nanda, Karina, Cecile, Kate, Klaudia and Jo

Despite the tone and tenor of your letter, I welcome your decision to send it and in so doing to take the initiative to engage in direct contact with me in a public forum such as this. You have obviously spent a great deal of time reading what I have written and have made an effort to respond to it in the midst of your busy study schedule. I am truly appreciative of this.

The tone of your letter is hostile, accusatory and peremptory. You start and end it without a salutation or friendly greeting. I look at this and wonder what response you were seeking to elicit by adopting such an approach.

Eye-witnesses report that one of the lessons taught by Hempfling to his Compact Schooling I students in 2010, a course which at least two of you attended together with Vicki, focused on preparations for communication with other people. Are you aware of what you are about to say before you say it and the response which it may elicit? Did you actually consider this before you wrote your letter to me?

My initial response was to reply to your letter with silence but then I read it again and was struck by a number of factors which suggested that a written reply would be more appropriate, one which should occur in the public forum that you have chosen: this blog.

The nature of your letter

So what are the factors that I refer to? In the first place, I am struck by the fact that you have sent me a letter which only deals with you in the last two sentences, and then only as an addendum to another person and organisation.

Secondly, I notice that your letter is predominantly concerned with what you perceive to be an attack by me against that other person and organisation rather than yourselves.

Thirdly, that person and organisation are Klaus Ferdinand Hempfling and his Akedah International school.

Fourthly, you are highly critical of me and not only utterly uncritical of Hempfling but describe him in terms usually reserved for a distinguished hero: "one of the greatest horse people and philosophers" and "so great, so honest, so authentic, so strong, so caring, so joyful and so respected".

Fifthly, I note that several turns of phrase are employed in your letter which are distinctly reminiscent of the style of English that is so typical of the flowery prose which is so frequently used by Hempfling himself.

Sixthly, I am aware that you have chosen to send me this letter in a public forum from Hempfling's school, where you are currently studying, and I am also aware that no communications written about or on behalf of Hempfling normally leave the latter or his school for publication in the public domain without his permission.

As such, I believe that there are eminently reasonable grounds for me to conclude that yours is a letter which, if not written in part by Hempfling, has been drawn up and sent on his behalf in your capacity as his utterly loyal, unquestioning followers with his consent to defend him and his interests, yet you only do so in so far as you are attending his school as his faithful students.

Your claims and accusations
Accordingly, I shall address you in the role that you have chosen for yourselves: loyal, unquestioning followers of the man you clearly acknowledge as master: Klaus Ferdinand Hempfling.

You start by stating that no part of this blog "has anything to do with the reality of this man and his teachings" but in the same breath you tell me that "you take all you can get out of him and his accomplishments for free, just as you please". These positions seem to be irreconcilable with each other. Perhaps you are confused as to which, if either, applies.

You claim that I once wanted something from Hempfling. Yes, it is true that I once wanted to attend the same course at Hempfling's school which you are about to complete. I entered into an agreement with him for this purpose, in accordance with which I undertook to pay him a large sum of money and he promised to teach me in return. I was prepared to keep my side of the bargain but was Hempfling willing to keep his promise? The fact that I am here and you are there speaks for itself.

You contend that I have taken things from Hempfling for free. Let me tell you that I have paid for everything that I have learned from him except where the relevant information has been offered freely by the man himself, any of his accredited coaches or anyone who has learned from him in the capacity of a student and/or an assistant. I have paid for his books, his DVDs and any paid publication or forum in which articles by or about him have appeared.

The "negative things"

In the same breath you accuse me of publishing "negative things" about Hempfling in this blog. Let us examine who is responsible for those negative things – your master, me or anyone else – as I run through the main ones that I have covered in this blog:

1. Vicki and I were denied entry into the one-year course which you are about to complete, because we refused to pay your master more than we had agreed to. Was I responsible for your master's actions in this respect or was he?

2. after Vicki and I were denied entry into the one-year course, your master invited us to his home in Denmark to start afresh and find a solution which would enable us to attend his school. We dropped everything and drove from the Netherlands to Denmark to do so, only to find that he was absolutely not interested in any solution but was more preoccupied with securing my submission to his will. Was I responsible for your master's actions in this respect or was he?

3. for a long period of time your master refused to refund my deposit of thousands of euros in accordance with his own general terms and conditions, finally doing so only after lengthy proceedings through the European Union's European Consumer Centre, when I threatened to turn to the courts to sue him not only for the refund of that deposit but for compensation based on breach of contract. Was I responsible for your master's actions in this respect or was he?

4. some time after your master's one-year course started, I discovered a German woman called Sigrid Kreile, who had spent some time in a sect in Catalonia, Spain, earlier this century and had suffered psychological abuse and financial loss in her efforts to escape from it. She wrote a book about her experiences called *Im Bannkreis des Pferdeschamanen* [Under the Spell of the Horse Shaman] which was published in 2005 (see my post entitled *Snippets Germane to Germany* in *In Search of the Master Who Dances with Horses:*

Growth). The leader of that sect was subsequently identified in the public domain as your master by various individuals, including one journalist and two psychologists. Was I responsible for your master's actions in this respect or was he?

5. your master promised to teach no more than ten students at a time as part of his one-year course but grossly exceeded that number by combining it with other courses during the period from September to November 2011, in September 2012 and again this year during his summer academy, which is now drawing to a close. Was I responsible for your master's actions in this respect or was he?

6. your master promised the one-year students free accommodation as advertised by him but chopped and changed that accommodation a number of times both before and during the course. Was I responsible for your master's actions in this respect or was he?

7. the majority of the horses that started the one-year course with you are no longer with you. One of those was Karina's young gelding, Cody, with whom your master failed to achieve a magical connection and whom Nanda later inexplicably wrote that she feared him (see my post entitled *Breaking the Cycle of Chaos* in *In Search of the Master Who Dances with Horses: Growth*). You know what happened to Cody and so do I. Was I responsible for your actions and those of your master in this respect and, if not, who was?

8. 30% of the students who started your one-year course have dropped out. Am I responsible for this?

9. your master gave you a promise in his advertising materials for his one-year course that you would have the opportunity to qualify as a body awareness and/or horse practitioner. The latter qualification (horse practitioner) is evidently no longer available. Am I responsible for your master's actions in this respect or is he?

10. about seven and a half months into your one-year course one of your fellow students, Jasmijn Wauters, left your master's school, abandoning the dream that had taken her there and running the risk of losing the fee she had paid for the remainder of the course which she missed in accordance with Akedah's general terms and conditions. I ask myself how much pressure she must have felt was being brought to bear on her to have taken such drastic action and risked such loss. Was I responsible for this and, if not, who was?

11. earlier this year Cecile, acting on behalf of your master's school, which you defend so passionately, contacted an equestrian centre where your former fellow student, Jasmijn Wauters, was scheduled to give a number of courses and effectively tried to have those courses cancelled. The excuse was lame: Jasmijn had mentioned that she had studied with your master for seven months in her advertising materials. Let us put this into perspective. Not only did Jasmijn study with your master for more than seven months, she was also the only student amongst you who worked with three different stallions while studying with your master, and was the only one amongst you whom your master evidently felt was good enough to feature in one of his YouTube videos while training a stallion (I am referring to training and not chasing a stallion away from a mare, which is what you did in the same video, Jo). Through Cecile your master's school endeavoured to prevent Jasmijn from doing part of the work she performs in order to earn a living. Was I responsible for this or was it Cecile, your master and/or his Akedah school?

12. your master relies on videos, images, stories and books depicting him as an excellent horseman to entice people to attend his courses, which until quite recently were predominantly geared towards teaching them body and spiritual awareness rather than learn how to interact with horses in the way that your master does. Am I responsible for this discrepancy or is your master?

13. not too long ago your master had new terms and conditions drawn up to govern the services which his Akedah school offers. They are strongly loaded in his and his school's favour and are potentially highly prejudicial to his students. Am I responsible for your master's actions in this respect or is he?

So I could go on, if I were to write more about your master and his school in this blog. And each time I would be able to ask you whether I am responsible for your master's actions or whether he is.

Seeking the external or the "inner guru"

Here I should stop to say that what I present as conjecture or speculation in my writings is precisely that. Equally, what I present as fact is not "guesswork" as you assert. Rather it is based on personal, frequently corroborated experience, written or other hard evidence, the testimony of eye witnesses or a combination thereof.

You claim that I want to be like this man, your master. After reading the numerous points that I have just mentioned, do you honestly believe that I seek to be like your master? And if I tell you that what I have mentioned is just the tip of the iceberg of what I know, do you really believe that I want to be like him "just once, one single time"?

If there was a single horseman whom I would like to resemble it would be a quietly spoken, unassuming man who lives with his wife and a small herd of horses in a rural area of the French-speaking state of Quebec in Canada. There this gentle man came to horses quite late in his life (at 37 years of age to be precise) but within the space of a decade he had managed to develop such a close relationship with horses that he was able to teach them collection on the ground using nothing more than a cordeo (neck ring) and a twig. He cares for his herd of horses in accordance with holistic principles and interacts with and trains them in the herd at liberty or only on a cordeo. His horses are free to join in the interaction or leave when they choose, as they are not confined by a small picadero (square version of a round pen) such as that used by Hempfling, a round yard such as that used by Parelli and other so-called " natural horsemanship" trainers, or even a large manège such as that used by Nevzorov. This is a man who empathises with horses and humans, who empowers them, who is enlightened in his approach to them, and who is trustworthy. Is he perfect? No. But I would dearly prefer my shortcomings to occur at the level that is his. The man's name is Michael Bevilacqua and he is so without ego, that he eschews the limelight and refuses to publish his profile on prominent websites, such as YouTube and Facebook. (Michael Bevilacqua has since opened a Facebook page using the title of his book.)

Yes, if there was a single horse person whom I would very much want to be like, it would be Michael Bevilacqua but I do not want this and there is a very good reason for it. If I have learned anything from your master and in spite of him, it is that I need to become not like him or anyone else but like myself, my true authentic self. This is the essence of your master's teachings, for it is only then that I will have a chance of becoming a human whom a horse seeks to be with.

You suggest that I only find negative things to write about your master. This is not true. If you read my writings and not merely scan them for what you believe to be "negative things" about your master, you will know that the positive things that I have written about your master far outweigh any mention of "negative" actions on the part of him and his school about which I have reported but for which, as I have shown above, I am not responsible. I do not doubt that your master is capable of being 'so great, so honest, so authentic, so strong, so caring, so joyful and so respected". All of us are capable of this. For most of us, including your master, it is a constant struggle to allow this capability to materialise and this is why I feel that I can identify with him more readily than with Michael Bevilacqua, to whom such qualities seem to come more naturally than to Hempfling or myself.

Acknowledgement of Hempfling's role

Your master has played and continues to play a major role in helping people rediscover their authenticity and, in so doing, become humans whom a horse seeks to be with. This in turn is of major benefit to the horses those people encounter in their lives. It is a role which has had a major impact on my life, first in providing me with the inspiration – through his magical relationship with his chestnut gelding, Janosch – which really set me off on this journey that started in 2007, and since then in what I have learned from him through the various avenues that I have mentioned above. And it is a role which I hope he will continue to play through his various printed and audio-visual publications, as well as his online presence.

Rediscovering your authentic self
When you look at yourself in the mirror each morning as you count down to the close of your one-year course at the end of this week, do you really see your authentic self or do you see your master peering over your shoulder urging you to do all that pleases him and to avoid all that displeases him, rather than what would bring you closer to your authentic self? And if you do see your master in the mirror, perhaps it is time – as you leave your master's school – for you to ask yourself whether you should not be doing what he preaches rather than what he wants. It is eminently possible for you to strike out on your own, and like those who have gone before you and are already doing so – yes, people like Noora Ehnqvist and your former fellow student, Jasmijn Wauters – draw and build on what you have learned from Hempfling. And if you do this, you will still be able to claim in your publicity materials that you have spent a year studying with the great Hempfling over a period of two years, for this is true and no one – not even the man whom you currently treat and praise as a perfect master – can take this away from you or deny your legal right to publicly acknowledge your teacher, whether he supports you or not.

Alternatively, you may choose to continue to serve as your master's loyal, unquestioning followers. Either way it is your choice and whatever you choose to do, I respect your choice and sincerely wish every single one of you the very best. May you eventually find within yourself the ability to become the kind of human a horse seeks to be with. I would like to leave you with the following words of wisdom:

> Ironically, taking time to observe and reflect instead of seeking answers outside of ourselves may bring us much closer to ourselves, horses, nature and what we want, than we ever imagined possible. In the world that we live, it can be one of the most difficult journeys to pursue. That fragile, subdued flame within our hearts struggles against the oppressive, surrounding norms. This is your chance to bring it back to life.
>
> (Michael Bevilacqua, *Beyond the Dream Horse*, p. 8)

Take care and be well, all of you, including your master!
Andrew

Becoming the Kind of Human a Horse Seeks to be With: Part 2
9 October 2013

On Friday, 27 September 2013 people from around Australia began to gather in the small town of Tallangatta on the banks of the state of Victoria's Lake Hume. Some brought horses with them, while others did not. What they all had in common though was that they could look their horses in the eye and say, "I am on your side". So the inaugural Corroboree Equus got under way and up to 22 humans got together to celebrate and share a new way of being with horses, listening to and learning from each other and their equines rather than any outside, self-proclaimed guru. And magic was created.

Waterfall Creek
Before we attended the corroboree, Vicki and I were privileged to be the guests of two of its three organisers, Glenn Wilson and Kelly Bick, at their lovely home and guesthouse situated on a 150-acre piece of paradise at Waterfall Creek in the beautiful Tallangatta Valley. As some of our regular readers may know, Kelly and Glenn have frequently left comments on this blog and it is through this that we made their acquaintance first online and later in the flesh. Their comments led us to believe that they are very special people. Their presence confirmed that this is indeed the case.

I was privileged to spend two hours on my own with their herd of thirteen horses, meditating on the natural beauty in which we found ourselves until several equines arrived at my side and were later joined or replaced by others. Often there is one that finds a way into your heart. This time it was a lovely little chestnut mare called Sonnet. Hesitant initially, she held herself slightly back as she viewed the reception which I accorded to her more forward grazing mate. Once reassured, she edged forward to hold her head by my side before gently nuzzling my proffered knuckles, and so began an hour of shared meditation, snuggles and scratches.

While Sonnet captured my affections, it was a regal Australian standard bred that held me in awe. Although clearly old and slow, the horse was fit, filled out and healthy at an age that commanded my respect: 40!

Inaugural Corroboree Equus

Even before it got under way, the Corroboree Equus was exceptional for a number of important reasons. First of all, no fee was payable, as anyone who felt that they were on the horse's side was entitled to attend free of charge. All one was required to do was to assume responsibility for one's own accommodation and food. Camping and kitchen facilities were available on-site for a nominal fee. Secondly, the programme was not structured around presentations given by publicly acknowledged gurus. Instead, the participants were responsible for their own content, with invitations extended to anyone to make a contribution, and many did. Thirdly, a multiplicity of disciplines were represented, meditation, Tai Chi, liberty training, equine-facilitated learning, positive reinforcement, friendship training and so forth. Fourthly, although there was a programme for the first few days of the corroboree, it is was not written in stone and could be changed, if and how the attendees required. They were the ones in control. Finally, all ages were represented, including mothers and their children.

The humans were joined by a variety of horses including three from Kelly and Glenn's Waterfall Creek estate, two horses belonging to their fellow organiser, Suzanne, a domesticated brumby – the name given to a feral horse in Australia – loved and cared for by a young girl in her early teens called Clare, and a mare owned by a friend of her mother, Linda. These horses featured in sessions covering meditation, liberty training, equine facilitated learning and positive reinforcement. Unfortunately, the horses were not allowed to share a field as a herd, as some of their owners felt that this might lead to an unsafe situation.

Becoming the kind of human...

A few weeks ago I mentioned that I would be giving a presentation at the corroboree entitled *Becoming the Kind of Human a Horse Seeks to be With*. In a post of the same name (Part 1) I presented our readers with a summary of some of the points that I was planning to raise during that presentation and requested feedback. Some of you contributed ideas, for which I am grateful and thank you accordingly. One of the points that some of you made was that horses in captivity do not have the freedom of choice available to their kind in the wild. Interestingly, in the course of my presentation at the corroboree, people felt that horses suffer constraints on their freedom of choice both in captivity and in the wild, even though they do differ somewhat.

As mentioned in my previous post on the subject, my presentation was to cover the things that we do together with our horses in the course of which we become a friend to them, the things we give them in our role as their protector and guide, and the qualities that we develop in ourselves in the absence of which those "things" may not be achievable and the horse may decline to seek the human. Rather than present everyone with a list of those qualities as I saw them, I endeavoured to get participants to identify them by viewing slow-motion stills from videos featuring Klaus Ferdinand Hempfling, in which the latter's posture, position and facial expression are clearly visible as he interacts with certain horses, establishing a clearly discernible close relationship with them. Based on those excerpts my audience was asked to list the qualities that they saw in Hempfling which enabled him to attract the various horses to him and to establish a connection with them. The qualities which they listed covered an entire sheet of butcher's paper and then some. In essence, they largely coincided with my own summary, which is as follows:

- contentment, relaxation and inner strength;

- trustworthiness and reliability;
- a capacity for empathy and empowerment;
- clarity and the ability to communicate;
- awareness, focus and intent;
- authenticity and intuition: presence in the here and now.

It would appear that these are the qualities that Hempfling possesses when interacting with some horses which enable him to become the kind of human those horses seek to be with. By extension they are also the qualities which we would need to develop within ourselves, if we wish to do the same.

Reply to Hempfling's One-year Student, Kate
14 October 2013

Kate, one of the Australian students attending Klaus Ferdinand Hempfling's one-year schooling course has responded to my reply to the remaining one-year students' letter (see my post entitled *Reply to Hempfling's One-year Students*) in this public forum. It is a reply which seeks to open channels of communication and which raises important issues concerning the relationship between people and self-proclaimed horse gurus in their quest to become a human whom a horse seeks to be with. Because I feel that this debate goes to the essence of some of the concerns which this blog seeks to address, I have decided to deal with Kate's letter in the form of a separate post.

Kate's letter

Andrew,

It is interesting, and accurate that you term Klaus a master.
It is a word that I was most nervous of at the start of my schooling.
The word did conjure up for me an assumed loss of individuality,
I pictured that I would have to go against myself in order to carry out someone else's wishes.

The common consensus with the One Year students was that I had lightning bolts coming out of my forehead toward Klaus when he was teaching in those first three months.
I was, then, a classic product of modern society.

In this day and age there is little room for (and quite a lot of fear of) the ancient structure of master and pupil as one did find so common in traditional times.
Masters were sought and honoured in music, martial arts, war, horsemanship, calligraphy etc.
If one did find the right master, who could prove himself

trustworthy, it was natural, and understood as necessary, to honour the masters guidance.

Nowadays with society so focused on the 'individual right' not the community or collective, there is a rapid fear around the idea of master and pupil.

The fear is so strong in some it is but a small jump in their minds to call this structure of master/pupil cult related.

Klaus never told me to cut it out with the lightning bolts in those early days...he always said to question everything. Never disengaged your own mind.

If one is to serve another, horse, human, nature, child...anything...it must be done without relinquishing yourself.

In our western society it is considered the individual's right to have his opinion.

In Klaus's school we are taught it is our duty.

Before every class begins, Klaus always asks...'does everyone agree? Does anyone not agree?'

As we are training authenticity and sensitivity, we train to increase the awareness of our inner sensations and of course these cannot exclude our opinions!

If we were to be mere puppets in Klaus's school, and mutely follow his word, we would be refusing the first major step toward authenticity.

It would be like someone wanting to learn how to fly but refusing to get in an aeroplane!

What is authenticity if not the seamless expression from inner realm to outer form with nothing limiting, stagnating, negating, over rating, expecting (I know it is not a word but it brings me great pleasure to leave it there in honour of the delightful European English of the One Year School) or castrating the organic nature of the being.

In the early days of the schooling I did try to be a good student, (a common legacy of our society) and when I took this approach to the horses it was repelling!

I remember one sweet mare was very fast to stand on her hind legs because I was trying to be good....and Klaus calling from the sidelines....'stop trying to be good! Stop pretending! Ground yourself, Kate. Be yourself!!

Thankfully those days of trying to be something other than myself in such a gross unconscious way are over.(the deepening of authenticity never over though, as my task and duty and delight in life continues.)
It is why I am so intensely grateful to have been a student of the One Year school.
(And threefold delighted that it took two years....)
To be authentic one has to strike out on a path where no one has been before.
It is simply not possible to walk in someone else's shoes to get there.
Klaus has always said 'You have to jump! Trust yourself and jump! Trust Life and jump!

It is the most valuable thing to day after day be offered the safety and encouragement to jump into your own waiting arms.
Such delicious simplicity, being yourself.
Trusting the Life that brings you to Life, animates you, breathes you.

It enjoys writing words like this....and then goes to bed.

Kate

KFH masterclass.

My reply
Dear Kate

In that your letter appears to be a genuine attempt at communication, it is most welcome. In that it addresses issues which go to the heart of some of the concerns addressed by this blog and does so through this public forum, I have elected to deal with it in the form of this post.

It is true that I have referred to Klaus Ferdinand Hempfling as "master" in my reply to the letter which you and the remaining one-year students addressed to me through this blog last month. You will recall that I did so in the context of the role which all of you assumed in that letter, namely, that of the loyal, unquestioning followers of the man whom you sought to defend in it. Within that context "master" merely denotes a person – in that case Hempfling – to whom you and your fellow students have chosen to be allegiant.

"Master"

You then continue with a discussion of a very different type of "master", one modelled on the bygone concept of a person (usually a man) who is an expert in his chosen field of activity and who assumes the role of teacher and protector in relation to those in his charge while they are training with him. It is pertinent that you do so, for it is precisely the type of master that I had in mind in the open letter which I sent to Hempfling on 26 May 2011, a copy of which the majority of the then prospective one-year students received, including you. In that letter I wrote the following:

> From the time when I first read your book, *Die Botschaft der Pferde* (*The Way of the Horse* – my version of the title and not a literal translation), several years ago, I have been aware that the relationship you seek between a teacher and student goes beyond what one finds in a modern classroom. As I understand it, the trust that you demand has more in common with that of the traditional European relationship between a master and his pupil, one that is complete in its commitment to teach and to learn. Essential to this compact between master and pupil is that the pupil must learn to walk through the darkness of the unknown trusting that his master will ultimately show him where to find the light. This is the trust that you refer to and you are right to do so.

You will note from that letter that I was already familiar with this notion of "master" which you refer to. You will also note that I was readily prepared to accept and abide by it for the purposes of Hempfling's one-year school. Not only did I not fear it, I actually embraced it! It should therefore come as no surprise to you that my familiarity with this concept of "master" enables me to avoid any confusion between it and the role assumed by a cult leader. You may therefore safely assume that I am quite capable of drawing a clear distinction between the two.

Just (fair) and trustworthy

So just what is this distinction in relation to trust? In your letter to me you cite a quality which you deem to be a prerequisite for it to be "natural and understood as necessary to honour the master's guidance". The quality that you refer to is trustworthiness. As you yourself put it, "it was natural and understood to be necessary to honour the guidance of a master", if one could find the right one "who could prove himself trustworthy" (your words). To this extent I would concur with you but I would suggest that trustworthiness is but one of the qualities required in such a "master". The other is that such a "master" must be just, that is, fair in his dealings with his students. As I put it in my open letter to Hempfling of 26 May 2011:

> There is another aspect to this compact between master and pupil which seems to have been neglected and it is this. The trust that the pupil needs to have in his master can only survive if it is based on justice. The traditional European relationship between a master and his pupil was based on the assumption that a master, however harsh, demanding or incomprehensible (to his pupil) his actions may be at any time, will always treat his pupil justly. A pupil was and is entitled to expect this. Justice is the rock on which the pupil's trust in his master stands tall. Without it, trust crumbles like dust into the quicksands of injustice…. If you want the trust of a pupil, do you not need to commit to the justice which makes a master precisely that: just and trustworthy?

The man to whom you ascribe the quality of trustworthiness is indeed capable of being just and trustworthy in his dealings with horses and humans, as we all are. I know this to be true in the case of some horses, as I have recognised it clearly in some of his videos and have recently given a presentation at the Corroboree Equus in Australia which dealt with this.

Yet I must also confess that I have personally experienced a distinct failure on the part of the man whom you describe as such a "master" to be just and trustworthy in his dealings me. Some of the ways in which this has occurred are described or alluded to in this blog, as is his betrayal of the trust placed in him by Vicki. She attended three courses with your "master"", and together with me co-hosted two body awareness weekends for his then sole senior body awareness coach and your fellow one-year student, Jo Ross, in our home – one of which you attended yourself – and gave up almost everything to attend his one-year school with you and the others. Since then I have met a growing number of people who have worked and/or studied with your "master" – as his student and/or assistant – who sincerely believe – rightly or wrongly – that they have good grounds to conclude that he was not just or trustworthy in his dealings with them. They include two of your former fellow one-year students.

At this point let me state unequivocally that it is not my intention to judge Klaus Ferdinand Hempfling or blacken his name. The man who looks back at him in the mirror every morning is quite capable of doing this without any assistance from me or anyone else. More to the point, whether he does so or not is his responsibility and not mine. I admire him for his commitment to rediscovering his authenticity and to battling his demons. It is a daily struggle – but hopefully a joyful one – with which I can identify. Rather, I seek to highlight the qualities of being just and trustworthy, for they are a *sine qua non* – without which nothing – in our relations with horses and humans.

Authentic self

In your letter you go on to describe the process of embracing one's authenticity in terms with which I can wholly concur: "to be authentic one has to strike out on a path where no one has been before", "to jump into your own waiting arms" and "trusting the life that brings you to life". Amen!

And yet I note that, even after describing this process of personal rediscovery in such uplifting terms, you close your letter by defining yourself not simply as Kate Long, the authentic being whom you claim to have become, but instead in terms of someone else ("KFH") and that person's training programme ("masterclass"). Given that you are a native speaker of English, it is also striking to see that your choice of paragraph structure, a fair amount of the language and/or some of the punctuation resembles that employed by your "master" – a German for whom English is a second language – in some of his emails to me. As I look at this, I also note your decision to eschew the use of a courteous salutation and close in your letter to me. In addition, I am conscious that you are also a signatory to the letter addressed to me by the remaining one-year students last month.

Cody and Jasmijn

As I ponder this, the shadows of a horse and human cast a dark silhouette across my view, blocking out the light behind them. They are creatures who are familiar to you, for you shared space and time with them during your master's one-year school. The horse is a young gelding called Cody (renamed "Jo-Jack" by your master). The human is a young Belgian woman called Jasmijn, your former fellow student.

Cody joined the one-year course as one of two equines belonging to your fellow one-year student, Karina (for more about Cody see my post entitled *Breaking the Cycle of Chaos* in *In Search of the Master Who Dances with Horses: Challenge*). He was a horse whom the human you refer to as "master" failed to engage in dance. He was a horse whom at least one of your fellow students incomprehensibly came to fear, a horse who inexplicably came to be so dangerous that he could not be rehabilitated, not even by such a great horseman as your "master". How was it possible for this placid creature, whom Vicki and I saw at Karina's before he went to the one-year school, to become such a dangerous beast within just a few months? When Cody was condemned to his fate, did you, your "master" or any of your fellow students just for a moment stop to ask yourselves whether you were not failing him by no longer being just (fair) and trustworthy in your relations with him?

Jasmijn was your fellow student for more than seven months. By all accounts she was also arguably the most proficient horse person amongst you students. When she presumably felt so much pressure being brought to bear on her that she felt the need to flee the one-year course, abandoning the dream for which she and her father had made such a major financial sacrifice, did you, your "master" or any of your fellow students just for a moment stop to ask yourselves whether you were not failing Jasmijn by no longer being just and trustworthy in your relations with her?

Pattern of behaviour

I cannot answer these questions for you, nor do I seek to judge you in relation to them. What strikes me about these two examples, my own experience and that of the other people whom I have mentioned above is that a clear pattern of behaviour appears to be discernible. It would seem that if a horse or human is to receive treatment based on a just and trustworthy approach, they will need to submit unquestioningly to the will of your "master", and the human will be required to refrain from any opinion or action which could contradict that will. It would appear that such treatment may be denied – and action may ensue – if this is not the case. You, the remaining seven one-your students, are testimony to this. You have shown yourselves to be such loyal and unquestioning followers of your "master" that you are prepared to launch an attack on anyone against whom you believe you need to defend him, as is evident from your letter to me last month.

This pattern is also evident in the one-year course which you have just completed. Of the ten original students 30% dropped out, the three youngest students I might add. You are quite familiar with the attitude adopted towards them by your "master" and do not need me to remind you of that, nor of his vilification of Vicki and myself with such frequency that I wonder how all of you managed to find time for that, when there were so many other more important issues requiring your attention.

Perhaps I am wrong...

Naturally, I may be entirely wrong. Perhaps next week or the week after I will discover a video on YouTube featuring your "master" dancing with a resurrected Cody, a young horse with whom your master visibly empathises, whom he clearly empowers and towards whom he is evidently just and trustworthy. Better still, perhaps the video will feature Cody dancing with his human, Karina, the woman who originally took her young gelding to the master who dances with horses in order to learn to do just that, both horse and human empowered by him.

Perhaps next week or the week after I will also hear that none of the one-year students or their "master" were involved in condemning Cody to his fate.

Perhaps next week or the week after I will hear that your master has publicly acknowledged the prowess of his former student, Jasmijn, and that he has decided to be just and trustworthy towards her and her father by agreeing to an amicable settlement with them, compensating them for the four and a half months of training which she missed and the dream which she abandoned. What pressure she must have felt under to even contemplate the prospect? How much more to act accordingly? Perhaps it would help if you were to ask your "master" whether he promised Jasmijn and her father an amicable settlement and whether he actually lived up to that promise.

Perhaps next week or the week after I will hear that the remaining one-year students cross-checked the answers provided by their "master" to these questions with the email correspondence received by Jasmijn and her father from him and his legal pit-bull in Germany. More importantly, perhaps I will hear that you and your six remaining fellow students will have evaluated your own role in relation to the pressure that Jasmijn must have felt.

Perhaps next week or the week after I will hear that all of you have had contact with Jasmijn and that you have reconciled any differences that you may have had with each other.

Perhaps next week or the week after I will hear that Cecile and your master's Akedah school have apologised to Jasmijn for attempting to deny her the right to earn a living (see my post entitled *Hempfling's Student: Casting off the Master's Shadow*), because she does not hide the fact that she studied with your master for more than seven months (being the only one of his one-year students to feature training a horse in any of his YouTube videos and the only one of them to train with him while working with three different stallions). Perhaps I will also hear that they have given Jasmijn an undertaking that they will never do this to her again.

Perhaps next week or the week after I will rejoice to hear that all of this has occurred and that I have consequently got it all wrong. Perhaps….

Be yourself

While sitting here contemplating your letter, I think back to the Sunday afternoon when I drove you to the airport in Coffs Harbour, Australia. We were discussing the KFH body awareness weekend which you had just attended in our home in Bellingen. I remember mentioning that I found you to be exceptionally observant when looking at horses and that you appeared to be particularly sensitive to what they reveal about themselves. I sincerely hope that you have not lost this ability and that you are able to extend it to humans as well, including any "master" who threatens to become more important in your dealings with horses and humans than your own internal guru.

The "Kate" whom I hope I am addressing is not anyone's student but first and foremost a woman who lives and acts in her own right as an independent and authentic human being, one who is also capable of empathising with and empowering the Codys and Jasmijns of the world. If this is the "Kate" whom I am writing to, I salute you and wish you the very best in everything you do. If you are not that "Kate", I do so anyway and pray that you will someday find the "Kate" that is you.

Be well and take care!
Andrew

Into the Herd

17 November 2013

There are times when life takes you up in its active arms and hurries you along, depriving you of moments for reflection, as humans, horses or other creatures pass you by in ever-changing situations and new ones take their place until, in the midst of this wild whirl, this audio-visual kaleidoscope of jumbled colours, shapes and sounds, an almost irrepressible moment comes when you call the merry-go-round to a halt and jump off. The seemingly haphazard array of creatures and circumstances retreats leaving a ripple of what has been, which gradually spreads and flattens into a pool of silence. And in that welcome quiet I take stock of all that has passed and realise that, however hectic it may have been, it has probably been nowhere nearly as immense and challenging as what Pip and Anaïs have just experienced, for they are gone ... to another country ... and into the herd.

Horses and humans in the Antipodes

Our month in the Antipodes probably represents the most active trip that Vicki and I have ever taken anywhere. As I mentioned in my post dealing with the first part of our trip to Australia (*Becoming the Kind of Human a Horse Seeks to be With: Part 2*), we met so many wonderful people at the Corroboree Equus in Tallangatta, Victoria, and were privileged to stay with Kelly and Glenn, a wonderful couple whom we got to know through this blog and two of the three organisers of the corroboree, at their beautiful 150-acre property at Waterfall Creek, where we met their herd of horses. From Tallangatta we headed north to a 300-acre property in the Southern Highlands in New South Wales belonging to two writer friends, Anne and Susan. Although Susan was not at home, we got to admire their impressive collection of Aboriginal art and to meet their horses, view their cattle and sheep, and spy on some wild kangaroos.

Our next stop was Tamworth, one of Australia's top horse centres and the Aussie capital of country and western music, where we caught up with Jody and Jeff on their 150-acre spread, where their herd of twenty-odd horses mingled with the local kangaroos at dusk and dawn. Vicki met Jody at Klaus Ferdinand Hempfling's Compact Schooling 1 course in 2010. In Tamworth we got to sleep in an old shearing shed with enough cracks and dark corners in which to accommodate all of the eleven most poisonous snakes in the world to which Australia is home. Our hosts assured us that it was still too cold at night for them to go on slither-about, so we stoically got into bed, which was a mattress on the floor (very comfortable I might add), and went about the business of sleeping. My morning shower took place outside behind a wooden door extending from shoulder to knee, which enabled me to view the horses in the fields while washing the suds off.

Heading north-east we arrived in Bellingen, the last place we lived before we left Australia in 2011. There we caught up with Joan and Lyndon on exactly the same chairs at precisely the same table at the outdoor cafe, where we had left them two and a half years ago. It is amazing how you can just pick up where you left off and carry on as though you have never been away.

The next couple of days we spent with Peggy and Heather, and their respective herds of horses a little further north just outside Coffs Harbour. Both women attended the body awareness weekends which we hosted in Bellingen in 2010 and 2011 (where Hempfling's then senior body awareness coach, Jo Ross, presided over the physical exercise sessions) and are Hempfling Compact Schooling veterans, Heather having notched up a total of five courses. I find it interesting to note that most of what they are doing with their horses occurs in spite and not because of what they learned with Hempfling. What has definitely remained though, is the focus on being present and in the moment while spending time with their horses.

A little less than three hours north we caught up with many of the people whom we had befriended while living on our horse property in Byron Shire. There we shared meals and spent precious time with most of those whom we had hoped to see and also managed to catch up with Susan at her holiday home in Brunswick Heads. It a great to see all the old faces again. Bellingen and Byron shires are also what I like to think of as oases of sanity in a crazy world. There is a very pronounced, almost palpable, generally accepted concern for the earth and all of the creatures who inhabit it. This is reflected in a critical but healthy embrace of life and its challenges, and a commitment to the use and consumption of earth-friendly products. The icing on the cake is the natural beauty to be found in both areas.

From Byron we edged north across the Queensland border for a flying emotional visit to our geldings before spending a pleasant evening with our former pet sitter, Marie. The following day we headed for Brisbane, where we spent another pleasant evening, this time in a Nepalese restaurant (a first for me) with Penka and Laila, two lovely women whom we had befriended at the Corroboree Equus. The next morning we flew to New Zealand to spend just under a week with friends.

Aotearoa

If there is a country that should change its name immediately, it is New Zealand. The Maori have a very apt name for the country which rolls off the tongue like a song: Aotearoa (land of the long, white cloud). Aesthetically it would be a definite improvement and would boost the islands' image as an exotic destination in much the same way that Australia has avoided being called New Holland, the name originally given to it by the first European explorers to encounter it (the Dutch).

Kiwi country was home to us for the first three and a half years following our emigration from the Netherlands in 1992, the same year in which our friends, Wim, Marga and their two daughters, Hedda and Lidewij, crossed to the other side of the world to start a new life. It was good to see them again, more so, because we could spend time with them in their own home living at their own pace. As in Australia, much of our time was spent reminiscing as we roamed the spaces that we had shared with our animals in the past, and admiring the natural beauty that passes for countryside in that part of the world. Unfortunately, our time in Aotearoa was confined to two places – Nelson and Wellington – but you could do far worse to miss them on any visit to the country.

Kaimanawa wild horses

While in Nelson Vicki and I had the opportunity to visit a relocated herd of Kaimanawa wild horses confined to a section of hilly slopes to the south-west of the city. The Kaimanawa are feral horses that normally roam in the desert area around the volcanoes in the centre of the North Island of New Zealand. For various reasons the authorities have decided to limit the number of Kaimanawa horses in that area to about 300. Any in excess of that number are culled.

Not too long ago a Spanish immigrant bought some land at the top of the South Island and resettled about twenty-five of those horses. The number has swelled to thirty-four but the stallion has since been gelded. We visited that herd and were amazed to see how well the horses had adapted from the poor pasture and undulating to rough countryside of their original habitat to the steep heights and relatively rich, grassy slopes of their new home. However, this has not occurred without any effects on the horses' health.

The boys

To me the absolute highlight of our trip to the Antipodes was being reunited with our geldings, Gulliver and Farinelli. Following our return from New Zealand we spent a week oscillating between visits to them and the people we still wanted to see in Byron Shire, where we were fortunate to be able to stay in Anne and Susan's holiday home. The boys are doing much better than we had expected. Being thoroughbreds, Vicki and I knew that it would be difficult to keep weight on them as they aged. Although this is largely true for Gulliver (and was already the case before we left Australia), we were pleasantly surprised to note Farinelli's condition. He has kept his weight and is moving relatively well for a twenty-year-old. At twenty-four, Gulliver is showing his age. However, both horses have shiny coats and look relatively content.

I had not expected the horses to miss us and this seemed to be confirmed by their response to our arrival. We barely merited a raised eyebrow. Yet in our interaction with the boys all of us slipped easily into familiar behaviour. Gulliver turned to us for head scratches, while Farinelli took to nuzzling our hands as he had been wont to do in the past. It was clear that, although they may not have missed us, they did appreciate our presence, although there was the odd misunderstanding on the part of both species too when we misread each other's body language. This I put down to the difficulty of trying to match old ways with new insights. Seeing the boys with all the space at their disposal also led me to give serious thought to the conditions in which our mares are required to live in the Netherlands. At the time they were on holiday at a natural horsemanship facility in Belgium. Perhaps we needed to leave them there for the time being.

Into a Belgian herd
Which is what we decided to do. Just before we left for Australia, we were told that the horses in our livery yard would only be allowed out of their stables during the winter if the weather permitted (which means, no rain or snow) and then only into the dressage arena, which would be cordoned off into tiny sections. This came hard on the heels of a rather traumatic accident involving a 10-year-old gelding belonging to the owner of the yard, which was accompanied by a great deal of suffering on the horse's part. The gelding had suffered an injury requiring major, costly surgery. The owner decided to have the horse killed (I am deliberately avoiding euphemisms such as "put him down"). It was decided not to bring a vet in to do the deed there and then (early evening) but to wait until the morning when he could be taken to the local abattoir, a cheaper option I am told. I offered to cross the border into Belgium to pick up easily available, cheap

painkillers outlawed in the Netherlands to help the gelding get through the night but my offer was turned down. The horse went to his death the next morning. By the time we heard about the winter regime a few days later we felt we had reason enough to consider not returning to that livery yard, so four months after we moved in we left.

Horses are kept very differently in our new livery yard just across the border in Belgium. There they live as part of a herd of 20 in an enclosed area of what must be about one acre and a bit (about 0.5 hectares), which has both indoor and outdoor sections. The horses are fed hay twice a day and have permanent access to straw. In addition, we give ours some hard feed and additives once a day. All of the horses are barefoot and none of them wear rugs. For six months of the year they also have access to various fields for grazing. The way I see it, our horses will not only be able to move when they like, they will also be living in more natural albeit not ideal conditions.

The spiritual nature of horses
Becoming part of the herd following their introductory holiday in a small, adjacent field with a walk-in shelter has been a pretty trying experience for our mares. Neither Pip nor Anaïs has experienced anything quite like it, although Anaïs has lived outdoors permanently with two other horses in the past. The mares had to contend with what passes for the local herd's version of a stallion (a dark, tank-like gelding) chasing them away from the feed. This went on for a couple of days but there were too many feeding posts for him to patrol, so our mares did not starve.

However, they have picked up a few cuts and bruises. During the first week Pip was befriended by a small, black Belgian warmblood called Billitis, who decided to protect her new friend against anyone. For her pains Billitis suffered a massive kick to the left hind leg, which has temporarily taken her out of the herd, and Pip suffered a manageable injury to her right hind leg. This has since healed but today when I last counted, Pip had three bite marks (one of them still open) on her right hindquarters, two on the right shoulder, one on the left-hand side of her neck, one on the left shoulder, two on the right hindquarters and a new one at the top of her right foreleg. For anyone who is floating around on a cloud contemplating the spiritual nature of horses, this is a reminder that nature can also be quite ruthless at times. Having said that, the New Zealand equine ethologist, Andy Beck, makes the point that horses usually only resort to violence with each other, if they feel a need to compete for available resources. We can see a few things in the yard in respect of which this would be the case, especially now during the colder months when the horses have less space available.

During the past week Pip has also started to walk unevenly, if she is not downright lame to begin with when I get her out of the enclosure. The owner of the yard tells us that it could have something to do with the fact that she is moving around on a harder surface than what she is accustomed to. There could be some truth to this, as Pip walks much more evenly on the grass, when I take her into the forest. Vicki and I are not too sure if the hardness of the surface is the only reason for her pain. It has been pretty wet here over the past month and we suspect that the mud and the water may be playing a role as well. Returning Pip to the enclosure this afternoon seemed to confirm this, for she immediately started walking as though she was trying to balance on bottle caps. For the time being I am playing it by ear. The rain has stopped and a dry patch has been forecast. We shall wait and see. In the meantime we are administering Equine Touch to both horses to help their bodies cope.

The next step
If you have been following this blog for the past couple of months, you will probably be aware that Vicki and I are contemplating our next step. We feel a need to reinvent ourselves and had been contemplating a move to another country as part of that step. This has been part of the reason for our trips to Spain and Australia in

recent months (see also my post entitled *Becoming the Kind of Human a Horse Seeks to be With: Part 1*).

While our mares have made their move with the result that we now have four horses in two different countries with ourselves in a third (a rather curious situation in anyone's book, I would imagine), Vicki and I have still not worked out where we should be heading, if at all. With its raw beauty, wide open spaces and pockets of sanity, such as Byron and Bellingen, Australia carries great appeal. I am mindful though that the last time we based a decision purely on the heart, it was to leave Australia to attend Klaus Ferdinand Hempfling's one year schooling course, a move which took a curious twist. Everything that had anything to do with travelling to Europe and settling there seemed to work out well, while anything that had anything to do with Hempfling's course started falling apart within two days after our arrival in the Netherlands.

I am mindful too that, as I have mentioned in this blog, one of the most important lessons which I have learned from that experience is to try and live more intuitively. By this I mean that I feel a need to be alive to what life (call it "destiny", the "universe" or whatever) is suggesting as it unfolds, rather than to ignore that and to try and run counter to it, as I have too often done in the past. There is a temptation to rely on analyses and comparisons, a trap that Vicki and I fell into when we emigrated to New Zealand in 1992 and ended up spending only three and a half of our nineteen years abroad in that country. Ultimately, analyses and comparisons may confirm or deny the sensibility of a course of action but the choice in favour of the latter needs to come from the gut. It has to be intuitive, acknowledging a force in our lives about which we understand so little because we are too intent on paying homage to the gods of rationalism, objectivism and empiricism, and dismiss everything outside their domain as unfit for intelligent beings.

Moving meditation
A little over a fortnight following our return from the Antipodes and our mares' entry into the herd, I find that I derive considerable

strength from my daily moving meditation, be it my morning Tai Chi sessions or afternoon interaction with Pip. Whatever the challenges that changing circumstances may bring, those sessions help me to achieve a sense of quiet contentment and acceptance that whatever will be will be, and it will be fine, however challenging.

For those of you who are also using Yang, Jwing-Ming's Tai Chi Chuan and Qigong DVD and printed learning materials, I can tell you that my morning sessions now start off with the warm-up exercises followed by the primary qigong set and then the fundamental eight stances. I now follow this up with Hempfling's three riding body awareness exercises (walk, trot and canter) as taught to me by his then senior body awareness coach, Jo Ross, and end with the Masai jump (which serves as a great release). In the future I will probably be heading more in the direction of Qigong than the classical Tai Chi sequence, because I find that it places me more effectively in the moment and helps to develop presence, which I then try to replicate when I am with the horses. I honestly believe that Pip has to contend with a more aware, observant, empathetic and empowering human as a result, one who is capable of giving her the support that she requires during one of the most challenging experiences of her life following her entry into the herd.

Lessons of Europe
22 December 2013

It is a wealthy continent with a rich history and arguably the most liberal political and personal freedoms in the world, yet it is also one whose so-called leaders, following largely in the footsteps of their US master, have a penchant for dictating what is right and wrong to the rest of the world, while striding through it like bygone warlords dispensing punishment and rewards as self-interest dictates albeit now under the guise of a self-proclaimed moral high road. On the horse front, it is also a continent of confronting paradoxes and challenges, something I have become very mindful of, as we try to overcome the vicissitudes of livery accommodation for our horses under your scrutiny and feedback, which can be as challenging as it is helpful. Yet Europe is also an arena in which I find that I am learning important lessons. This time I would like to share some of them with you.

Out of the herd

As I mentioned in my last post, *Into the Herd*, Pip had gone lame. Over on the other side of the world, Glenn put on his thinking cap and, reviewing his own experience, suggested that the problem could lie in the possibility that "Pip might be suffering from thrush/bugs deep in the central sulcus of the frog – which can make them tender footed, especially on hard ground – but is quite a subtle problem as in general the hoof looks fine, with just a slightly deeper CS [central sulcus] groove".

Although the right fore hoof, which is where Pip was most tender, did look fine and had the healthiest frog, I decided to go with this suggestion from the other side of the world and started to treat the hoof with NT-Dry and, lo and behold, Pip started to walk better.

Leave it to the witch doctor

By that stage, however, I had decided to play it safe and bring in a vet, as one does when one believes that one requires expert advice and assistance. Although Vicki and I felt that the problem was in the hoof and were convinced that it was not in the upper leg or body, we could not rule out the pastern or fetlock and this is where we felt a vet could be of some assistance. Perhaps, after more than two and a half years back in a part of the world where people have as much faith (I use the word very advisedly) in modern doctors as their forefathers had in the European equivalent of witch doctors (part of a tradition with which I became familiar during my formative years in Africa), I was beginning to succumb to the same influence.

Beguiled I must have been, for she was young, blonde, attractive, intelligent and authoritative. It sounds like a sorry excuse but it is the only one I can come up with. But why do I refer to it as an excuse? Simply because I found myself accepting and doing things the mere thought of which I would not normally entertain. It started with the examination of Pip's foot. That examination commenced with a lameness test, which entailed that I was to take a lame horse in pain and force it to trot on a hard surface after bending its hoof up against its lower leg for a short period of time. Then I was asked to trot Pip in a circle on a surface which was so uneven that I would not even have contemplated doing so if she was sound. Oh, and while we were at it, could I please trot her several times on the same circle with first only the hoof anaesthetised and then both the hoof and the lower leg to the fetlock. All of this was done in the name of diagnosis and by the end of it the vet had not even inspected the hoof.

Accepting responsibility

The vet left and I suddenly realised what I had done to Pip. Not only had I forced her to trot in pain, worse I had also insisted on trotting her under local anaesthetic. While I can fully comprehend the need to track down the problem, I cannot understand why there is a need to trot a lame horse in pain for so long when a few steps are really all that is required to establish that there is pain and where the source is likely to be located. Without a close inspection of the hoof and advanced technology, such as X-rays and ultrasound, trotting a horse in pain simply remains guesswork and only really causes the horse to suffer more than it already is. I knew that Pip was going to be very sore when the anaesthetic wore off and I suspected that it would get worse over the next few days. And I was absolutely livid with myself for abdicating my responsibility to my horse simply because a vet insisted that I do so.

Unfortunately, I was right on both accounts. Pip was in far worse pain than she had been before the vet arrived and the condition of the foot deteriorated over the next few days. Fortunately, that vet had left me with several sachets of "bute", an anti-inflammatory and moderate painkiller which is banned in the Netherlands but is fortunately available in Belgium, where our horses are currently in livery. This helped to some extent, although Pip was not keen on the taste and it required some lateral thinking to get the stuff into her. Now it was time to live up to my responsibility towards her.

Not in the hoof?
Although the vet was convinced that the problem was not in the hoof, I still had my doubts. For a start, there were a few soft spots and small black stains on the sole and a number of tiny holes had begun to show up in them. The hoof had also begun to smell. Equally convincing was the treatment that I had started before the vet came. It had seemed to help. Accordingly, I decided to operate on the assumption that we might be dealing with an abscess and Vicki and I began to bathe Pip's hoof in warm soda water twice a day, one of us popping over the border in the morning and the other in the evening. In addition, I decided to remove Pip from the herd and she is now in a separate enclosure and next door to the other horses with its own large, walk-in walk-out shelter. Taking her out of the herd has enabled her to relax and to start coping with a situation which had really cast a blanket of gloom around her.

This time we also brought in a professional barefoot trimmer to inspect the hoof and advise us. He cut away most of the black and soft spots, while opening up the tiny holes to check underneath. All he found was healthy sole. To play it safe I also arranged with the vet to come back and take x-rays. Much to my astonishment, I actually had to insist on having the hoof x-rayed as well. If nothing else, we have ruled out bone problems. At the age of sixteen, Pip has the clean joints of a four-year-old. This time the vet left us with about ten sachets of "bute" and I wryly reflected that we were likely to receive a pretty hefty bill for two lengthy visits, one of which required the presence of a second vet to take care of the radiology, and that all that Pip had actually received in the way of medical assistance had been sachets of an anti-inflammatory. This is not to say that I have no respect for conventional medicine. Conventional veterinary medicine has saved the lives of a number of our animals in the past. What I have learned though was a lesson that I had assumed I had already learned before: I am responsible for my horse and no one else.

Pip in boots
Since the vet's second visit I have been bathing Pip's hoof in soda every day and she has been making remarkable progress. I have trimmed her hooves and this has also seemed to help. There is no sign of any abscess or the likelihood that one will form. Pip is now able to trot, canter and even jump for joy on soft ground. She is walking well on asphalt, although she is still a bit sensitive at the trot. In the past couple of days I have noticed that she has a flap of sole that is beginning to be dislodged as new sole grows underneath. The only drawback we have experienced on the road to convalescence is that we have had to take Anaïs out of the herd and place her with Pip, to prevent the latter from running to and fro. As Pip recovers, the mares are beginning to grow bored and appear to be keen to rejoin the herd.

It seems to me that Glenn was right. After having lived all of her life on soft ground with metal shoes initially but in recent years none, Pip's front hooves must have been placed under enormous stress, when she suddenly found herself having to negotiate very hard surfaces. I had assumed that, because she had been barefoot for some time, she would be able to cope. What I had not counted on was that her weak right fore hoof would be more susceptible, a situation compounded by the fact that we have had one of the wettest autumns in recorded memory. The excess water must have softened the hoof and made it more vulnerable to the hard surface, which abraded parts of the sole allowing bacteria in.

At the end of next week we are planning to reintroduce our mares into the herd. This time though I want Pip to be prepared. I have bought her some jogging shoes. No, I kid you not. They are flexible shoes which offer protection without inhibiting the hoof mechanism and they were invented here in Europe, in Norway. Not only are they used for hoof remedial work but they also feature as protective footwear for endurance rides, showjumping and even dressage. And here in the Benelux, where regular visits from the farrier can empty your wallet rather rapidly, such jogging shoes are a far more affordable, not to mention healthier, alternative. My idea is to have Pip wear these jogging shoes on her front feet for part of the day until her hoof grows strong again. Then we shall take them off and see how she fares.

Life in livery

Life in livery is a challenge not only for our horses but also for their humans. Since we placed Anaïs in livery here in the Benelux in May 2011, we are now in our third different establishment and each of them has had their challenges. It is a solution that is far from perfect but one which many people find inevitable for some or other reason. The challenge lies in accepting that, however convenient this may be for the human, it does not excuse the human from their responsibility for their horse. If we accept a horse into our lives, we also need to accept that, with the exception of not being directly responsible for its accommodation and much of its feed, we are responsible for every other aspect of its well-being.

Having said that, I look back on our experience in Australia, where we owned two different horse properties. To be sure, it was great to have our horses with us, to be able to go out and be with them at any time of the day or night. Yet in such a theoretically ideal situation we also had major challenges to contend with. Our life in the subtropics meant high rainfall and rapid-growth subtropical grasses. As a result, we had to find ways to deal with frequent abscesses and the danger of the horses developing "big head" due to calcium deficiency, to name two of the major challenges that we faced at the time. Put another way, having your horses at home with you instead of in livery does not mean that you will not be faced with challenges. At the end of the day, whether your horse is in livery or at home with you, it is like everything else in life: how do you deal with it? With a groan or with a smile?

Humility
Rita's call to us to accept responsibility for our horses in her comment on my last post has led me to reflect not only on that responsibility but also on our inability to be sensitive towards other people and the different situations within which they find themselves. On our last horse property in Australia we ultimately managed to set up an infrastructure and create conditions which allowed our horses to live in a herd and to do so happily and safely. Our fencing consisted of polymer coated high tensile steel cables with a breaking strength of 600 kg secured to recycled plastic posts which were flexible to about 30°. We had three large fields covering several acres, each with their own large walk-in walk-out shelter with their entrances facing away from the direction of the bad weather. To counter the mud we laid gravel in all of the high-traffic areas, which also had the effect of strengthening our horses' hooves. It took us ages to achieve this and we learnt a lot in the process.

Coming to the Netherlands has challenged many of the basic assumptions that I had developed in the process. Here we have more than sixteen million people and half a million horses living on the equivalent of two of Australia's largest sheep stations. Space is at a premium and the rain has nowhere to drain off to on the flat land. Horses are kept very differently as a result. During the summer they go out in the field during the day and are stabled at night. In most cases they are confined to their stables or sand paddocks during the day in the winter, because the fields are too wet, frozen or snowbound. And if they are turned out, the fields are soon churned up into mud, which is why many horses are not turned out when it rains. It is all very well to come in from Australia and proclaim that horses should be kept the way we were used to keeping them. In most cases it is not an option here in the Netherlands or Flanders and certainly not in a livery yard. Perhaps some humility is required to resist the urge to barge in hurling condemnations with self-righteous zeal.

We have constantly sought to ensure the best available facilities for our horses and, given the extraordinary circumstances in which we started out in our new livery yard, we are not yet prepared to condemn it simply on the basis of an unfortunate start. Sure, eighteen horses (two have since left) on one and a half acres in the winter is really pushing it but viewed within the Dutch and Flemish context our livery yard does not represent such a silly compromise. Instead of being confined to stables or a small sand paddock (often an outdoor arena or smaller), every horse has the option of utilising all of the space available and, because they are kept in a herd, their constant interaction with each other means that they move much more than they would in a stable or paddock. In addition, the horses do not depend on this space for their feed for the simple reason that grazing outdoors would not yield sufficient nutritional value in the colder months, even if they had access to fields. Instead they have constant access to quality straw and are fed hay at regular intervals throughout the day.

The next big step is small
For some time now Vicki and I have been discussing the need to reinvent ourselves. We feel that we have closed a chapter and are now ready for the next big step. For many weeks now we have

thrown ideas around and have tried to understand the direction in which our life has been moving. We have now started to take the next big step and it is a small one. For the time being we will be staying where we are and will start doing the things that we feel are important. How that pans out will probably lead us to the next small part of our next big step.

Amongst other things, we have resurrected our Equine Touch studies, which have lain dormant for a while. This afternoon I hope to complete my last case study for Level 3. Then there is a fair amount of theory to study and a couple of related assignments to complete. If all goes well, we hope to do our Level 3 exam at the beginning of February. This will leave us with just sixty case studies to do with twenty different horses before we qualify as practitioners, hopefully by June.

Horses, Herd, Hooves, Horseshoes, Hempfling
18 January 2014

There is something appealing about alliteration. It must be the repetitive sound as the words roll off the tongue. Then there is the way the mind is focused on their individual meaning. The sounds may be similar but do the words semantically belong together? At first glance these seem to. After all, they all seem to have something to do with horses. Of course, some might argue that horses are no longer kept in a herd, while others might assert that horseshoes have no business being on hooves, while still others who have attended a course with Hempfling might claim that he is opposed to horses not having shoes or being kept in a herd. Whatever the case, these are the words that define this post, so let us just get on with it.

Recovery and relapse
In my last post I mentioned that we had removed Pip from the herd to give her hoof a chance to recover and that Anaïs had to join her, to prevent her from fretting and running up and down. I had started to use NT-Dry fight the bacteria in Pip's right forehoof to recover and she was convalescing well. I had also bought her a pair of jogging shoes for her scheduled re-entry into the herd.

Vicki and I were very fortunate to have the opportunity to spend the week of Christmas with her twin sister, Agathe, and the latter's partner, Ron, in a large country house on the outskirts of Mijas on the Costa del Sol in southern Spain with a small herd of horses including Agathe's mare, Ochet, in a stable complex next door. There we enjoyed good company and warm temperatures with the exception of Christmas day, when we were hammered by a storm, which was so severe that we had to bring the local pooch indoors. Poor Carmen was so distraught that she knocked over the chair on which my brand new leather jacket was hanging and promptly proceeded to devour the collar. And here I was thinking that dogs preferred meat rather than the container in which it is housed. Fortunately, the travel insurance paid out in full so ultimately no real harm was done.

Less fortunate was the fact that upon our return I discovered that Pip had suffered a minor relapse. Belgium had been inundated with rain and the mares were standing in puddles of water and urine. Infection in a vulnerable hoof was virtually inevitable. Of course, this made it clear to me that we were not dealing with anything other than an infection in the hoof despite our vet's lofty (and ultimately expensive ... for us) theories to the contrary, so there was no reason why the mares could not return to the herd while Pip recovered, especially now that we had shoes for her to wear.

Back into the herd with shoes

Because our mares had been located in a small enclosure just next to the huge barn to which the herd has access, they still managed to maintain some contact with the other horses. This meant that their reintroduction into the herd proceeded with significantly less drama than the first time round. Apart from one or two minor nicks and scratches, our equine ladies have come through fine and the herd has settled down into an uneventful routine. Pip's front feet initially posed a challenge when it came to the jogging shoes. Because her heels are much lower on the right, she required a size 14 to accommodate the lower bulbs but the same size was too big for the left hoof, because it is higher on the heel. I ended up having to order a second pair of boots a size smaller. This however turned out to be a blessing rather than the curse I initially thought it was.

Here in the Benelux we have been experiencing unseasonably warm weather with plenty of rain. Conditions in the herd enclosure are consequently much wetter than normal. Pip's jogging shoes go on in the late afternoon and come off in the morning, so she is wearing them about 15 hours a day. Because we have two pairs to work with, I can take one lot home to dry out on the heater, while she wears the other. I apply NT-Dry when I put on the shoes and they allow the powder to do its healing work, while simultaneously protecting Pip's hooves as they grow stronger.

Rediscovering the hoof

The theory that a horse's hooves will adjust to the conditions in which it finds itself remains very much that, an idea which may or may not be convincing, until you actually see for yourself what an amazing living organism a hoof is. Since our mares have been in their new surroundings in Belgium with a surface that is much harder than what they were accustomed to in the Netherlands, I have been watching their hooves adjust to these more demanding conditions. And now that we are successfully treating Pip's vulnerable forehoof, I am seeing these changes in that hoof as well. It is like rediscovering the hoof. Whereas our mares hobbled around as though treading on glowing embers in the beginning, they are now both walking out without any sign of tenderness and are even managing to trot with ease over the hard centre of the indoor arena. I look at their hooves and I can see why. The soles have become significantly thicker, even that of Pip's right forehoof. If you want to check how thick a horse's sole is, look at the groove around the point of the frog closest to the toe. That is the thinnest part of the sole. As a rule of thumb, the deeper the groove is, the thicker the sole.

Yes, Pip is still wearing her shoes everyday or should I say was. Yesterday we discovered that the steel buckle had broken off one of the shoes without tearing the strong nylon to which it was attached. It would appear that we are dealing with a faulty buckle rather than a structural flaw in the shoe. What it means though is that, until we can get a replacement (a great test of our warranty rights), Pip will only be able to wear shoes every other day. Part of me is wondering whether this is not simply what should be happening anyway, because my mare has been making such amazing progress. Interestingly enough, I have just discovered that in the meantime a new version of these shoes has been released. Called the Equine Fusion Ultimate, it has no external ties or buckles and it is made of a material which is better able to withstand wet conditions. Something for the future perhaps.

Kiss my shoes

Klaus Ferdinand Hempfling is a firm believer in horseshoes. I never thought that I would ever confess that I am too. There is a place for horseshoes in the hoof convalescence process or where a horse requires additional protection when jumping, for instance, or negotiating rocky terrain. Of course, what Hempfling and I mean when we talk about horseshoes, is where we differ. The Oxford Dictionary is going to have to update its definition as well. Given what the Norwegians are doing, the current definition of "a shoe for a horse formed of a narrow band of iron in the form of an extended circular arc and secured to the hoof with nails" is obsolete.

At this point in time I cannot think of a single legitimate reason from the horse's point of view why anyone would want to hammer a metal shoe onto the live organism that is a horse's hoof. We now have flexible shoes that provide protection when it is required and which can be removed when it is not. The shoes are easily cleaned by hosing them down or they can be tossed into a washing machine. They represent a solution which is not only convenient but which is also far cheaper than the six-to-eight weekly visits of a farrier. Of course you cannot leave them on permanently but why would you want to? For human convenience perhaps? But is that a good enough reason for your equine buddy, the creature you claim to love?

Equine Touch

Our Equine Touch studies are surging ahead. Vicki and I have just completed our Level 3 theory and practical components. At the beginning of February we will be attending the Level 3 course for the third time to brush up before taking the Level 3 exam at the end of the course. This means that we are having to practice and our horses are the lucky recipients of our attention. Pip has never been a likely candidate to become an Equine Touch junkie. More times than not she has refused to allow either of us to perform ET on her. This I have attributed to her readily excitable nature. In the past week to ten days, however, Vicki and I have been noticing a major change in my mare. She has calmed down significantly and my contact with her has grown noticeably closer. I suspect that her health care regime has something to do with it. She has experienced considerable pain and I have been helping her to recover every single day for many weeks now. It is as though she knows this, that I am there for her. Our bond is deepening as a result. Perhaps she is ready for more ET now.

Training and riding

Because of the major improvement in Pip's feet, I have resumed our 'straightness training" or what I prefer to call body balancing. Wherever they are and whatever they are doing, the mares normally come to us when we call them from the gate to the herd enclosure. Pip usually also comes to me when I call her to start a new activity in the manège. She seems to be enjoying a resumption of our former routine but our contact and understanding of each other is now much closer.

It is my hope that Pip will allow me to start riding her in the not too distant future. Once I feel that she is capable of carrying me without suffering any injury, I intend to ask her and see how she responds. If she makes it clear that she is not happy with the idea, I will stop. If she allows me to ride her, I will do so without a bit and only in measured doses. It is not my intention to burden her with more than she wishes to accept, which means that I will have to give her the freedom to express her displeasure if she feels inclined to do so. This is an approach which is not much different from the one that I am employing now as we continue to help Pip develop her strength and learn to move straight, while having fun together.

Equine Touch and Towards Riding

15 February 2014

February is hurtling along at a pace of knots, my days are fiercely full, and I am flying on a high. How is this remotely possible, you might ask, if you learn that we are coursing through what may go down in the statistics as one of the warmest, wettest winters in recorded memory, experiencing howling winds and pelting rain which should keep the sane indoors? Of course there is always someone worse off, our poor neighbours in England, for example. What doesn't flood, submerge and tear through their homes and lives goes on to pummel us here in the Netherlands as we deal with their weather leftovers. Of course, it's all the North Americans' fault. If they weren't hogging all the cold, we might have had a decently frozen winter after all.

Level 3 done and dusted

Not that I am complaining. On the contrary. Vicki and I are recently back from that saturated land (Glastonbury, Somerset) across the ditch (the English Channel), where we attended an Equine Touch practical course, before completing all requirements for Level 3. The course itself was one of the best we have attended. A largish group of predominantly women (I was the token male) with a wicked sense of humour ensured that it was as fun-filled as it was educational. To them I am grateful, as I am to our instructor, Lyn Palmer, and to the many horses with their issues who allowed us to help them, as we learned to improve our Equine Touch skills and did our practical assessment.

Vicki and I have just been informed that we have successfully completed all requirements for Equine Touch Level 3, which includes theory, anatomy, physiology, case assessments featuring two Equine Touch sessions on ten different horses in addition to our practical assessment. Apparently we have obtained ridiculously high marks and have secured unprecedented praise, which I personally cannot reconcile with my actual performance. Still, it is great to receive confirmation from those with greater expertise and more extensive experience, that we are definitely on the right track and are making good progress.

It was also good to be back in Glastonbury. It is such a quaint, alternative place featuring shops with gloriously whacky names. Vicki and I find it difficult not to think of our time in Byron Shire, Australia, whenever we are in Glastonbury. Another oasis of sanity in a crazy world.

Towards practitioner status

Back home, Vicki and I are now heading down the final straight towards the status of Equine Touch practitioner. In between everyday work and our daily visits to our own horses we are fitting in Equine Touch sessions with other people's equines. This time we need to prepare detailed case studies covering three sessions with twenty different horses. In addition, we need to complete three lots of written work: theory, anatomy and physiology, and an essay. Our target is June, when we hope to head over to England for a Level 4 course with Ivana Ruddock, one of the founders of the Equine Touch Foundation.

All in all, it is a highly educational if not sometimes an exceedingly frustrating experience. Shortly before we went to England for our Level 3 course and assessment, I accompanied Vicki to a stable around the corner from us, where she performed Equine Touch on a beautiful five-year-old mare. There various so-called sport horses are kept in stables 24 hours a day, their only outings being a daily ride in a manège and a session in a horse walker. The same saddle is used for all of the horses (I kid you not) and they are ridden in typical Dutch dressage fashion: pull the neck into a frame with the head behind the bit so that the crest rather than the poll is the highest point and then ride the animal into the bit, a bit like driving a car with the brakes on. For reasons beyond me, the owner could not understand why the mare was experiencing physical difficulties in its withers, shoulder and neck, as a result of which she was "playing up", which could mean her premature death if it is not resolved ("unusable" sports horses are often euthanised, even if they are otherwise healthy and would be healthier if allowed to live as horses).

Before leaving for England, Vicki had advised the owner to have the saddle checked and to seek the advice of a skilled, professional saddle fitter. Following our return all communications from her to the owner have met with a loud silence. Fortunately, for every sad story there are at least a few brighter ones. We are seeing progress in most, if not all, of the horses that we are privileged to help. Of course, Equine Touch on its own is not enough and neither is veterinary care. Perhaps the greatest need that we have, if we are to help horses, is not to put our hands on them but to educate their owners. Jock Ruddock, the other founder of the Equine Touch Foundation had a vision which is reflected in the foundation's mission statement: *helping horses by educating humans*. Amen!

Recovery
In my last post (*Horses, Herd, Hooves, Horseshoes, Hempfling*) I mentioned that a buckle had broken on one of Pip's horse shoes (meaning shoes horses as opposed to metal studs on their hooves), that this meant that she was only wearing shoes every other day, and that this was probably meant to be. This is confirmed by Pip's full recovery. I watch in awe as her right forehoof is changing before my eyes. The sole is growing thicker and there is increased concavity. As a result Pip is standing and walking straighter and more upright, and she is alive and alert again.

The difficult period that Pip has experienced in the past few months has also produced significant benefits. Both Vicki and I have noticed a major change in her. She has come to rest and has abandoned most of her anxiety. In my interaction with Pip I also notice that we now have a far closer bond, as though I have finally earned her trust, that she feels secure with me. This is reflected not only in our general interaction with each other but also in our training together. In this I am reminded of the two great mentors whom I frequently referred to in this blog. It is Klaus Ferdinand Hempfling who regularly points out that a horse will only give you its trust, if you can help it feel secure, although I don't for a moment believe that it is a question of just a few moments during the initial encounter in the case of most horses, as he would have us believe. And it is Michael Bevilacqua who makes it very clear that "understanding and trust have nothing to do with training".

Towards riding
Once you have that understanding and trust, however, then the training can begin in earnest. One of Hempfling's strengths is his insistence that riding is not the be and end all of the relationship between horse and human. Rather, it is the icing on the cake, the apex of a huge pyramid representing different types of interaction between the species. We may or may not get to it. Whether we do or not is nowhere nearly as important as the journey towards it.

Pip and I are on that journey. If it is meant to be, I hope to be riding her within a few months and to do so without metal in the mouth or on the feet (hers and mine). I am developing a holistic regime which involves an array of activities and supporting involvements, and which is designed to facilitate this journey. In a nutshell it involves all of the following (and every single aspect is essential if I am ever to ride Pip without injuring her):

- horse-friendly accommodation – working within the confines that are the reality here in the Benelux, Pip is able to move and feed throughout the day while socialising with her own species;
- beneficial nutrition – in addition to full-time access to rough feed, Pip receives appropriate hard feed and supplements;
- proper dental care;
- remedial trimming – under the guidance of a professional barefoot trimmer, I am working towards balancing Pip's front hooves;

- Equine Touch;
- preparation of the human – learning what a horse is, what it requires if it is to be healthy, discovering how it moves, so as to be able to help it improve its overall condition, losing weight (the lighter I am, the better for Pip) learning how to act in the moment, learning how to centre and ground myself to improve my balance and communication, learning how to breathe properly, learning how to use my body to communicate, learning the importance of connection, feeling and intent so that my interaction with the horse moves beyond being a mechanical affair to the extent that when I ask something of the horse, I also feel what I ask and the horse picks up on the energy of that feeling, knowing more precisely what I mean than if I merely resort to physical tools and aids;
- preparation together with the horse on the ground – as the Hempflings and Bevilacquas of the world have shown, this is the starting point for riding together with the preparation of the human. Without it, I would go so far as to say, expect to experience problems, major ones.

Like any programme, of course, it is just a plan and, as such, it is open to change.

The period ahead

In the period ahead I hope to share with you the types of activities that Pip and I will be involved in, the progress that we are making, the setbacks if there are any, and anything else which comes to mind. Some of you are further on this journey than I am. If you have any feedback, any ideas, tips, anything, I would really like to hear them. Never before in my life have I ever attempted to do something like this. It is a daunting prospect, a challenging one but I feel alive and, if Pip's responses are anything to go by, so does she. Perhaps after all of this preparation I will never get to ride Pip but that is also fine.

Towards Riding 1: The Horse
19 March 2014

It was a bit of a toss-up, determining where to start on the question of riding. My instinct tells me that Klaus Ferdinand Hempfling is right: you start with the human and not the horse, for ultimately it is the human that needs to change and to rediscover what it is to be human if they are to be of any value to the horse. On the other hand, the horse already knows how to be a horse and has not lost that knowledge of its species as we have of ours. Yet in the absence of the horse, a human has no need to consider the matter of riding, a realisation which seems to suggest that the horse must nevertheless be mentioned first, for it is the *sine qua non* (without which nothing) of riding. So let us turn to the horse in the first of this series of posts dedicated to the preparations which Pip and I are undertaking towards riding.

What is a horse?
Gosh, what a dumb question! We all know what a horse is, don't we. It is a "solid-hoofed plant-eating domesticated mammal with a flowing mane and tail, used for riding, racing, and to carry and pull loads" (Oxford online dictionary at http://www.oxforddictionaries.com/definition/english/horse?q=horse) or a "large animal that is used for riding and for carrying and pulling things" (Merriam-Webster online dictionary at http://www.merriam-webster.com/dictionary/horse). So there you have it. Let us take the common denominator of these definitions from the most authoritative dictionaries of the English language: a horse is a domesticated animal used for riding, and carrying and pulling loads.

Which means that, if you did not have any idea what a horse was before you read either of these definitions, once you had, you might only expect to see a horse with bits of metal, rope and/or leather about its body to enable humans to ride it or get it to carry or pull a load. If you want to get to know horses better, you would probably start out by visiting a riding school, where your initiation would start through an interface made up of your bum and the horse's back. Odds are that this is probably how you started out with horses, if you did not grow up in a family that keeps them. But if you did, the chances are pretty high that the bulk of your relationship with a horse has developed through that very same interface.

Doesn't it come with tack on?

In fact, most people who spend time with horses and have come to learn about them can probably trace much if not most of their knowledge of *equus caballus* back to that interface of bum and back. You learn about the tack you need to keep your bum on the horse's back and the training you require to do the very same while learning how to make the horse do things while your bum is on its back. Indeed, you may even go further and learn about the accommodation, feed and care a horse should have in order to be able to bear your bum on its back.

If you are really keen, you may even learn a bit about the biomechanics of a horse, which will enable you to "train it" to such a high level that you can make it do spectacular moves while your bum is firmly ensconced on its back. Indeed most of us who spend time with horses will probably know of few ways of spending that time with a horse other than with our bum on its back, and if we do manage to find another way, it is usually merely designed to enable us to do just that but with greater finesse.

We should therefore be excused if we fail to comprehend how anyone could walk with a horse on a lead in a forest instead of being seated on its back (a lack of comprehension which numerous riders have expressed to Vicki and myself when they have encountered us walking next to Anaïs and Pip in the forest). Indeed, we might even be excused if we have difficulty visualising a horse without tack on its body, a saddle on its back and metal studs on its hooves. Doesn't a horse come with tack and metal studs on it?

The light comes on at fifty

This is more or less how horses came into my life as a teenager. I knew nothing about them other than that many of my friends owned one and that every now and then I was given the opportunity to ride one of them. Someone taught me the basics of how to keep my bum on the horse's back when it moved, and how to make it move while my bum was on its back. This stood me in good stead on the odd occasions when a horse bolted under me, although it was not much help the day Gulliver and I encountered a wallaby (a smaller "version" of a kangaroo) in Australia. Good old Gulliver instilled in me the knowledge that a horse is a creature of flight, the lesson being learned the moment he veered out of the path of the skippy and I kept on going straight without a horse's back underneath me and landed on my head. Fortunately, I was wearing a helmet. I may have been macho in my younger days but I was not comfortable with the idea of dying (let alone "being") stupid.

And so horses drifted in and out of my life as creatures with whom a relationship could be developed through my bum and their back, until I lost interest in about 2002. Yes, I was prepared to help Vicki with our two geldings, Gulliver and Farinelli, when work commitments allowed but I was no longer interested in riding or doing anything else with them or any horse really. I could simply no longer see the point of making another creature do something for me, especially one with whom I did not seem to have much affinity and only really appreciated as another member of our menagerie (we had four dogs and three cats at the time) and fellow earth inhabitant.

It was in the year when I turned fifty, that everything changed. I discovered Nevzorov (and through him Michael Bevilacqua later on) and Klaus Ferdinand Hempfling. In ways peculiar to them these people inspired me to set off on a journey which, amongst other things, has led me to discover horses for what they are and not merely what we humans would like them to be. It is a journey that has revealed what other humans have discovered about horses but more importantly it is one that has allowed me to develop the skills and ability to start learning what horses offer us for discovery about themselves and ultimately what we can discover through them about ourselves.

Horses before humans

In a sense Nevzorov, Bevilacqua and Hempfling (and later Imke Spilker, Frédéric Pignon, Carolyn Resnick, Mark Rashid and Linda Kohanov) made it possible for me to start seeing horses as they are before humans exert their influence over them. It became clear to me that they are exceptionally sociable, seeking safety and security in relationships with other horses both as members of the same equine community and as close friends with another horse in the same herd. They are also creatures that are highly sensitive to and equally perceptive of an array of stimuli that are visible and invisible, audible and inaudible, tangible and intangible, and are capable of responding intuitively to them. In addition, they prefer collaboration and cooperation to the disquieting effects of conflict (with the exception of stallions competing for mares or where resources are scarce in relation to the size of the herd). It has also become clear to me that horses are capable of bonding closely with humans and those in captivity rely on us entirely to have their physical, emotional and other needs met, while acquiescing in or enjoying our guidance. To this extent, but only to this extent, we are the dominant species and, as such, we have the challenge conferred on us to empathise with horses, to be enlightened in our dealings with them, and to empower them, rather than to dominate them for our own selfish purposes.

These perceptions and deductions have since been confirmed by further study, for it is my belief that I should not aspire to riding a creature in the absence of instruments of force – that is, placing my trust in the horse to the extent that I unconditionally put my aging bones at its mercy – without understanding its nature. High on the list of studies recommended for anyone seriously wanting to understand the essential nature of the horse must be the work of the New Zealand ethologist, Andy Beck, and the cinematographer,

Ginger Kathrens. Based on an ongoing, long-term study, Beck's *Horsonality* (available at http://www.equine-behavior.com/Down loads/ppp.htm)is a work that no one who is serious about spending time with horses should neglect to read. Nor should such a person forego the opportunity to watch Kathrens' enormously informative and entertaining *Cloud* trilogy, the story of a stallion and the horses around him in the Arrowhead Mountains of Montana in the United States of America.

Yet there is another aspect which needs to be mentioned, because it explains why of all the animals on the earth, the horse has held an appeal for humans over the centuries beyond its role as a beast of burden which is more widespread and extends to more profound spheres of human endeavour than any other. In the course of time the horse has featured prominently in human politics, religion, sport and imagination as expressed in the arts and iconography, and still does to a significant extent today. At a personal level the horse is also arguably the only animal species with which humans can interact in a way that is capable of generating a nobility and beauty which is greater than the sum created by the two species doing what they might otherwise do best together on their own.

Safe, secure and at home
In his YouTube videos, *Immediate Connecting with Horses: 1* and *2* (you can view them at https://www.youtube.com/watch?v= 7uENNppDNJg and http://www.youtube.com/watch?v= zvuzDWleWeU) Hempfling notes what I feel is so important, that I wish to quote it here. Speaking about the connection he achieves with a horse during his first encounter with it, he states that to get a…

> positive response from the horse immediately means that I have to have a kind of unspoken contract with the horse. And this means, for example, that I will do everything not anyhow to hurt you, and I promise you to be on the maximum of peace in whatever I am going to do. I'm promising you that I'm going to take care that I will not be doing anything, not a simple step

> which is not in accordance with your proper individual growing.
>
> I'm the one who has to lead. There is no doubt about it. I have to lead in accordance with the needs and with the nature of the horse: give him safety, give him everything he needs to feel at home.

Whether or not you agree with Hempfling's claim that he manages to connect immediately with every horse that he encounters for the first time – there is evidence that he does with most of the horses he chooses to encounter and evidence is also available to the effect that he fails to do so with a small proportion of the horses that he selects – is utterly irrelevant for our purposes. What is relevant is the essence of what he states, a lesson which Pip has personally been trying to teach me since April 2012 and which she finally managed to do in January this year (some of us are hard learners).

That lesson is this: if you truly want to achieve a true, magical connection with your horse on a lasting basis, you will have to do everything in your power to show through your actions that your horse is safe and secure enough with you to be able to relax and be itself, which is simply its way of expressing its trust in you. It is my belief that anyone can make a horse move and some of us are far better doing that than others. The true challenge though lies not in making the horse do something but in the human finding it within themselves to encourage the horse to want to join in the dance with us, to become a willing partner. This, if I correctly understand the Nevzorovs, Bevilacquas and Hempflings of the world and the other guides whom I have cited, is the true goal of training. Yet without that true, magical connection it will be impossible to achieve that goal and without the horse feeling safe, secure and at home with you, it will not be able to trust you and that connection will remain an unattainable aspiration.

So what?

So what does this mean to Pip and me, as we continue our preparations for riding? In a nutshell, it means that before I can even begin to contemplate preparations for riding, Pip needs to be a happy, healthy horse in mind and in body. She needs to feel so safe, secure and at home with me that she will trust me enough to go along with anything that I ask, which she might initially feel is utterly alien and inappropriate, and that she will trust me enough to know that I truly do not seek to ask more of her than she is willing and able to give.

So how can I gauge the progress that we are making in this respect? Simple. Pip shows me. She has shown me that she is healthy. I look at her neck and see that the short, hard muscles which she had when she came into my life have given way to long, loose muscles which give her greater flexibility. My mare's feet have also improved. Not only has her hoof healed but she is now also capable of negotiating the hardest surfaces without any pain or discomfort. In addition, she is straighter and more balanced when she stands and walks. Pip now stands square and upright, and when she walks she now overtracks (the toe of her hind foot lands beyond the print of the toe of her fore foot) on both sides instead of only on the left.

The evidence is also discernible in Pip's attitude towards life and me. She is no longer that anxious bundle of nerves she used to be. Instead, she is more self-assured, is moving up the ranks in the herd and is even beginning to challenge Anaïs on occasion. Pip and Anaïs are part of a herd of eighteen horses that have been living together relatively uneventfully for some five months now. When Vicki and I arrive at the yard, either or both of us normally call to the horses from the entrance to the horse enclosure and our mares simply come to us. In the past Anaïs used to initiate the action and arrive first. Now it is Pip. In fact, on many occasions she recognises my tread on the pebbles close to the gate before she sees me and often arrives at the entrance before I have even looked around to find her.

Putting Pip on a pedestal
Another example. Vicki has taught Anaïs to stand on a pedestal. For ages I had tried to do the same but every time Pip simply walked off almost shaking her head as if to say, "You're crazy". As I mentioned

in my previous post, caring for Pip while she was having problems with her hoof was a watershed experience for us. Her attitude towards me changed completely. I did not realise just to what extent it had, until I took her to the pedestal, put my foot on it and uttered the cue, "Step", as I had vainly done so many times before, and she lifted her hoof slightly. I then bent down and raised it on to the edge of the pedestal to show her what I meant and then we tried the whole thing again. This time Pip simply put her foot on the pedestal and turned her head towards me as if to say, "Oh that's what you want? Well, here you are then." I could not believe it.

But more was still to come. A few days later I took Pip to watch Anaïs put both front feet on the pedestal but my mare did not seem to be overly impressed. A week later I discovered why. Asking Pip to put one foot up onto the pedestal and trying not to expect anything, my mare looked at me, turned back to the pedestal and simply stepped up onto it with both front feet. The next time I asked her a week later, she promptly walked right up and over the thing.

Is Pip ready for preparations for riding? I do not think that I am putting her on a pedestal when I say, "I think so". Of course, although I am hoping to start riding Pip next month, I am aware that I may never do so for one reason or another, for instance if she declines to have my bum on her back. At the beginning of April Pip and I will have been together for two years. Next month we will also both celebrate our respective birthdays. She will turn 17 and I will be 57. It is not the youngest age to contemplate a new start and certainly not one which envisages riding without metal in the mouth or on the feet. With the exception of the odd occasion on which Vicki has sat on her for a few minutes at a time in the manège, Pip will not have felt a human bum on her back for a little over two years. I have not had my bum on a horse's back for more than ten years. There are moments when I suspect that sanity has deserted me. But then a consoling thought comes to me: even though I may never get to ride Pip, it sure is great preparing to do so. For both of us, I think.

Towards Riding 2 – To Ride or Not to Ride?
16 April 2014

My last post (*Towards Riding 1 – The Horse*) elicited two comments which have profoundly affected my thoughts in the past few weeks and in doing so have helped create the basis for this post. The first comment came from Peggy on the east coast of Australia and it is this: "if you have a bond with your horse, are kind, considerate and don't ask too much too soon … that is it in a nutshell". The second was from Jade, who lives at the other end of the continent in Western Australia, and she wrote, "I have been thinking a lot lately about the horses' pain and riding and through working with a local equine Bowen therapist, I have realised that horses having some degree of muscle soreness or pain is generally accepted as a part of them being ridden. And the more I think about it, the more I realise that I have not come across one regularly ridden horse that does not have pain somewhere in the body, which scares me greatly. Now I'm on the search to see whether there are ways to prevent this." At first glance these two comments appear to reflect views at opposite ends of the spectrum. More importantly, they seem to imply a need to examine an underlying question whose profundity is all too often glossed over if not simply ignored: To ride or not to ride? This is the question.

The old and the new
Peggy is a dear friend who has often commented on this blog and who opened her home to Vicki and myself again during our trip to Australia and New Zealand in September and October last year. While we stayed with her, we were again privileged to witness the close bond that she enjoys with her horses and the extent to which they trust her. Older than we are and with vastly more experience of horses, to me Peggy represents a bit of what we humans have lost in our relationship with horses: the older generation's ability to enjoy a

no-nonsense, both-feet-firmly-on-the-ground, bullshit-free relationship with horses which is guided by genuine care and concern, albeit based on the assumption that riding is an essential part of that relationship to the extent that it is possible and enjoyable to engage in that activity while treating horses fairly and respectfully.

Jade is a young woman whom I have never met but whose inquiring mind and youthful wisdom stunned me when I first encountered her presence through this blog at the beginning of last year. So astounded was I that I promptly devoted a post to the story of Jade and her horses, Cisco and Dougie, and the revelations which it elicited within me. Entitled *Stillness in the Brumby's Breath*, that post serves as an appropriate background to this discussion along with my last post, which essentially deals with a human's awareness of the nature of the horse.

To me Jade represents part of the new generation of horse-loving humans who no longer wish to take everything for granted in their dealings with horses, in particular, the assumption that the driving force of the relationship between our species is the interaction between a horse's back and a human's bum. Jade opens her comment on my previous post with this introductory statement: "I have been following your posts closely lately because I have been contemplating the ethics of asking horses to carry us on their back, amongst other things we ask of them." The question, "To ride or not to ride?", is implicit in this comment. Has anyone you know ever asked themselves this question before placing their buttocks firmly and squarely on a horse's back and assuming that their "equine friend" has undertaken to carry them? Have you? Have I? Is it not a question that we should ask ourselves instead of assuming that our horse wants to carry us or insisting that it has a duty to do so?

Those who say "No"

There are humans whom I am aware of who have come to answer the question, "To ride or not to ride?" with a resounding "No". What makes their answer worth listening to is the fact that they include some of the most accomplished horse people of our time, humans

135

who have not only demonstrated their ability to train and ride a horse but who have managed to do so without resorting to instruments of force in order to do so, relying instead on their commitment to developing a close relationship with their equine friends, as part of which the horse becomes a willing partner rather than a servile subordinate in the interaction between the species.

Alexander Nevzorov used to be one of the most proficient horsemen on the planet, capable of helping a thoroughbred stallion and mare to learn and want to perform *haute ecole* (high school dressage) at a level comparable to that of the Spanish School of Riding in Vienna, Austria, the Cadre Noir in Saumur, France, and the Portuguese School of Equestrian Art in Lisbon, Portugal, and doing so with nothing more than a cordeo (neck rope) and a twig. Committed to a scientific approach towards understanding the horse and a passionate defender of the species' right to a life devoid of pain and suffering at the hands of humans, Nevzorov advocated riding for no more than ten to fifteen minutes at a time, before eventually concluding that even this compromised a horse's health. He therefore decided to stop riding completely.

In Canada the Nevzorov Haute Ecole's international representative, Michael Bevilacqua, a horseman with, as I understand it, an essentially different approach towards horses, one exhibiting more of an intuitive rather than a scientific bent, has come to a similar conclusion. Unlike Nevzorov, who received extensive classical dressage training before evolving his own horse-friendly approach, Michael Bevilacqua came to horses relatively late in life and had already developed a sensitivity and intuitive style by that stage, enabling him to move much more quickly than most towards developing a force-free, mutually empowering approach towards horses which allowed his equine friends to become willing partners in their dances together with him.

Another one-time NHE member, Stormy May, has also renounced horse riding. Famous for her release of *Path of the Horse*, a video documentary which has done much to encourage many humans to consider a new way of being with horses, Stormy May's story is special in that she used to be a traditional, successful trainer of horses and humans (including other trainers) in what passed for the art of dressage at competition level using a full array of instruments of force, metal and otherwise.

The burden of riding

So why have these humans, who have not only played such an exceptional role in helping others discover a new, horse-friendly way of being and interacting with humans, but have also demonstrated their own proficiency in helping horses to become willing partners in their own training, decided to abandon riding? Much of the answer to this question is to be found in what they have discovered about the effects of riding on the horse and the tools employed to facilitate that pastime, such as bits, bitless head gear, saddles and various instruments of force. Another part is to be found in the mental and physical condition of the horse, and the posture which it is forced to adopt when a human climbs on its back.

Bits

Over the years various experiments and studies have been carried out by different individuals and organisations into the impact of using common riding equipment such as bits, bitless head gear and saddles. For instance, Robert Cook, PhD., a graduate of the Royal Veterinary College in London, United Kingdom and Professor of Surgery Emeritus at Tufts University, Massachusetts in the United States of America, is a veterinarian who has extensively researched the carnage caused by bits over the years and has developed his own version of a bitless bridle to address his findings. You can read more about his work by visiting his website at www.bitlessbridle.com, where you will also have access to the numerous articles which he has written on the subject, including a paper entitled *A Method for Measuring Bit-Induced Pain and Distress in the Ridden Horse*), which he presented at the Ninth International Equitation Science Conference in July last year.

The Nevzorov Haute Ecole Research Centre is another organisation which has overseen studies by medical professionals into the effects of bits. One such study involved an experiment into the use of force applied by drawing on the reins or jerking them using a snaffle and a curb bit and featuring three different individuals: a 13-year-old boy, a 23-year-old woman, and a 43-year-old man. The experiment found that the following force was exerted *per square centimetre* of the horse's mouth in contact with the bit:

- 50 kg to 100 kg when the reins were drawn (not pulled);
- 180 kg to 220 kg when the reins were jerked with average force;
- more than 300 kg in the case of a strong jerk.

Not much in the way of imagination is required to picture the impact of such force on the sensitive surface of a horse's mouth. You can find more information about this type of research in Alexander Nevzorov's book, *The Horse Crucified and Risen*.

Bitless

Nevzorov has also written about the effects of using bitless head gear, such as a hackamore, side-pull, bosal, mediakana, cavasson, kapcung, or Parelli or other brand of rope halter. You can find more information on this in the anthology produced by Nevzorov Haute Ecole and edited by Lydia Nevzorova entitled *Equestrian Sport: Secrets of the "Art"*.

Saddles

Stormy May has studied some of the work carried out by professionals, such as the saddle-fitting expert, Dr Joyce Harman. A number of studies have been conducted into the effects of riding on a horse's back. Stormy May presents the findings of some of the more pertinent ones in Chapter 3 of her book, *The Path of the Horse: From Competition to Compassion* and quotes Harman's conclusion to the effect that "Pressures that exceed 0.75 psi will close down the blood flow in the arterial capillary bed" of the horse's back, because that is the highest blood pressure found in that area. The best saddles that Harman found in her study were graded at 1.93 psi, which is more than twice the pressure required to cut off the blood flow in the capillaries of the back. According to Harman, studies of canine and human muscles have revealed that sustained pressure of a mere 0.68 psi for over two hours can cause significant superficial tissue damage as well.

Of course, saddle pressure does not only manifest itself on the surface of the horse's back. It is actually transferred through the muscles to the bony structures. Stormy May quotes Harman as stating that, "There is surgical evidence in human medicine that subcutaneous necrosis [the death of cells] begins closer to the bone before cutaneous redness and ulceration is seen". Transposed to the equine condition, this means that white spots or tender swelling in the saddle area are the end results of a long process of shallow and deep tissue destruction.

Interestingly enough, the effects of saddle stress need not be confined to the saddle area. A poor-fitting saddle may cause pain in the shoulder, withers and lumbar region but the effects may even manifest themselves as pain in the neck. If a horse hollows its back to escape discomfort or pain in the saddle area, there is a very good chance that it will suffer pain in the brachiocephalicus muscle, that thick, long muscle that runs along the lower part of the neck up to the atlas vertebra near the poll.

Other instruments of force
Not much imagination is required to understand the use and effects of other instruments of force, such as spurs, whips and the numerous physical restraints and devices which humans have invented to compel the horse to do what they want or to prevent the horse from doing what it wishes. They simply have no place in any healthy relationship between horses and humans.

Physical condition
If a horse is to carry itself properly, it needs to be physically fit enough to carry itself. To carry a human a horse also needs to be fit

and strong enough to carry the additional weight and put up with its movements, and to achieve a posture that will facilitate this (see *Posture* below). If I would like to ride Pip, the very least I need to do is to ensure that she is healthy, that her feet and teeth are properly looked after, that she develops appropriate musculature and flexibility, that she walks straight and is able to carry herself. This is a prerequisite for a physically healthy life in herself and, as such, must come before any contemplation of riding. It is simply what you would do if you care for your equine friend.

Expecting Pip to carry me if she is physically unable to do so comfortably, would be tantamount to knowingly and wittingly deciding to inflict pain on my horse every time I climb on her back. Would I do this to a friend I claim I love? The situation is made more difficult by the fact that Pip has suffered severe tissue damage during her life, if the large white marks on her withers are anything to go by. Will she be able to carry me without hurting herself?

Mental condition

There is much talk of sports horses being bred to have the keen temperament which is required for top sport, with the result that they are edgy, nervous and easily excitable. To a certain extent this is true. To a large extent it is an apology for the very conditions that humans force sports horses to live in, which are ultimately largely responsible for that very nature. Many if not most sports horses are deprived of the opportunity to live like a horse, being permanently stabled with their only respite from full-time imprisonment in a small cell (aka. stable) being a few hours of training or movement in a walker each day.

Trainers such as Nevzorov, Bevilacqua and Klaus Ferdinand Hempfling have shown that it is quite possible to train horses to perform supremely difficult physical feats without reducing them to potentially dangerous bundles of anxiety. Pip was trained and competed up to a fairly high intermediate level here in the Netherlands, which is another way of saying that for many years she was chased into the bit while largely off-balance and having her neck painfully bent as her head was pulled towards her chest in what passes for dressage in this country. The result was a mental condition that reflected the physical trauma of riding. Utterly insecure and unsure of herself, she used to be an inconsolably anxious mess when divested of the physical trappings of horse-human contact that she was accustomed to and is still prone to seeking escape in blind speed, if she feels remotely threatened. In addition, although she has not really been ridden for more than two years now and has no pain in her shoulders, she still goes through the motions of nervously nipping when I stoop to pick up her front feet, especially on the right, where she used to place the bulk of her weight.

Will Pip be mentally prepared to accept me on her back? More importantly, will she be willing to do so? I have absolutely no idea. What I do know is that I must be prepared for the fact that she will not.

Posture

A horse carries most of its weight on its front legs. Without a human on its back, this does not represent too much of a problem. Put a human on its back and it will start to carry more weight on its front legs and its shoulders than what it can comfortably support. And if that human is unable to synchronise with the horse's movements, the situation will be immensely exacerbated and the horse will suffer more.

It is for this reason that classical dressage was developed. The theory is that by training horse and human, it will be possible for the rider to learn to synchronise their movements with the horse while simultaneously helping the horse to raise the base of its chest and to bring its hind legs further underneath its body, thereby shifting the centre of gravity more towards the rear to redistribute the weight of horse and human more evenly over its feet. The process is called self-collection or self-carriage (the horse collects and carries itself naturally) and if it is done properly it should start from the rear and move to the front arguably leaving the head to find its own position.

As Nevzorov, Bevilacqua and Hempfling have shown, this requires training which allows the horse to seek the posture of collection rather than have the human force the horse into a frame. As such, it is very different from what you will see at dressage competitions at all levels, where the horse is essentially pulled into a frame and ridden into the bit, somewhat like accelerating a car with the brakes on. It is not for nothing that the FEI (the supreme body of equestrian sport) insists that riders use double bridles on their horses at the higher levels of competition. The awesome leverage which those devices employ makes it possible for humans to exert great pressure on the horse's head with a minimum of effort. Remove those instruments of force and you will see very few humans who are capable of riding their horses in self-collection. Indeed, if self-carriage were to become the criterion by which dressage is judged, it is likely that equestrian sport as we know it would not survive in the absence of enough humans capable of helping a horse achieve it.

Personal proof

As you may be aware, Vicki and I are currently performing Equine Touch on horses as part of our final case studies en route to becoming practitioners. By the time we are qualified we will have performed 120 Equine Touch sessions, excluding the many other horses that we have had the privilege of helping without doing so for the purposes of our studies.

When I view the detailed case notes that I have taken for all of those Equine Touch sessions, it is difficult not to conclude that riding inflicts pain on horses in most cases. An Equine Touch session does not involve a human coming in and carrying out a treatment on a horse. It is an interactive session during which we feel and watch the horse, learning from the animal just how it feels and responds to what we are doing.

I have performed Equine Touch on stallions, mares and geldings of a variety of breeds from calm Shetland ponies to stressed 18-hand warmblood sports horses involved in a diversity of activities from recreational riding to jumping and classical dressage. In the majority of cases the horse has shown me that it is in pain, often in the back and/or withers but predominantly in the neck and/or shoulders. I have also tried to help owners help their horses by suggesting that they get the hooves, teeth and saddles tended to. Many have done so. Others have not. Yet even where these potential problem areas are eliminated, the pain frequently returns after every ride.

Concealing the evidence

Horses excel when it comes to concealing pain or rather learning to cope with it. If they are generally treated fairly by a caring human, they are more likely to tolerate the discomfort when it occurs. Others become passive victims acquiring the learned helplessness associated with that condition. Still others resist but this is usually a one-way street to annihilation, once they are classed as "dangerous".

Yes, it may be true that in the case of sports horses we try and stretch the animal to achieve the next level. After all, this is what we humans do when we engage in sport. I am not against horses being involved in sport. Many enjoy it. But really, should I not be asking myself whether I have the right to inflict pain on my horse in pursuit of a sport that I have chosen to indulge in, through which my ego and wallet may benefit and in relation to which my horse has absolutely no choice?

Really nice, friendly humans

So what about the humans? Surely they must be monsters, if they regularly inflict pain on the creatures they claim to love? Absolutely not! At the risk of sounding downright condescending, my experience is that, with the exception of the odd horse dealer whom I have had to contend with, the owners of the horses on which I have performed Equine Touch are really nice, friendly humans who, on the whole, want the best for their horses.

So why do I regularly end up performing Equine Touch on horses that are ridden into pain every week? Why do I regularly see horses being ridden that do not have the musculature and general physical condition to support the demands being made of them or whose hooves are in such a terrible state that it is simply a question of time before they start to experience issues in other parts of their body if they have not begun to do so already? What is it that makes a really nice, friendly human do this to the horse they claim to love?

A large part of the answer lies in ignorance. The vast majority of horse owners or riders simply are not aware of the nature of the beast that they ride. Inherent in that ignorance is the dark truth that we humans have been accepting the abnormal in our horses as quite normal for far too long. "Oh, my horse usually does that...." "Yes, my horse can be a bit naughty...." "No, it's just that my horse is normally sensitive around the poll...." "Yes, my horse always shies away from the bridle...." "Oh, my horse usually nips when I tighten the girth...." Sound familiar?

Of methods, techniques, devices and other madness

So what is to be done, if anything? At times such as this one may be tempted to look for solutions in the form of methods, techniques, devices and anything else resembling madness. If all of them are merely designed to cause the horse to do something rather than elicit our equine friend's commitment to being part of the solution, we may want to give that avenue a miss.

Naturally, we may then be tempted to consider the approaches adopted by those we respect for recognising the horse's innate ability to be a partner rather than a pawn. Should we look for guidance to Mark Rashid who rides with a bit and a Western saddle responsible for pressure way in excess of what is required to close down the blood flow in a horse's back, yet who is probably more sensitive to his horse's needs than most? What about Hempfling, who rides bitless with a cavasson and a loose rein but who trains in a picadero of 11-15 m by 11-15 m and insists that the only way forward is that of destiny, his? Perhaps we should be emulating Nevzorov, who once vociferously castigated anyone for relying on any equipment other than a cordeo and a twig, and a training area smaller than a sizeable church? Or should we be sitting at the feet of Chuck Mintzlaff, who condemns Bevilacqua for being just another

Nevzorov lackey who relies on equipment and a confined space whereas he can do without either, albeit without providing an answer to the question begged as to just how he hopes to help a horse collect itself enough to support a rider in trot and canter without compromising its health?

Stormy May suggests an alternative to everything and all. For this reason it is worth quoting her extensively:

> Now the problem with riding has been detailed, let's look at possible solutions. First, we must understand why we want to ride a horse. If the answers include, "it's fun" "I want to compete" or "it's good exercise" then the previous information will have little or no impact on what you do and the current horse world will give you plenty of support in pursuing your goals. If your answers sound more like, "I love horses" "I want to learn how to have a good relationship with my horse" or even "I think horses might have something to teach me" then it's likely you've already started to look for alternatives to the traditional horse world.
>
> (*Path of the Horse*, p. 33)

It is in the eye

And just what do those alternatives entail? Again, Stormy May suggests an answer to this question:

> The solution has to begin with the premise that the horse knows her own mind, and in any matter regarding her behavior, she is the authority. Horses don't have a spoken language we can understand but they do have a language we can learn. It is a language of physiology and movement. Once we spend enough time letting go of what we think we know about horses, we leave space for "what is" to reveal itself.
>
> (*Path of the Horse*, p. 33)

Although this statement is essentially true, there is one caveat that must be mentioned. Horses may suffer from trauma-induced muscle memory, which is another way of saying that a past trauma may have induced a physical response in the horse which is still evident in its behaviour even though the original condition that triggered it may have long since healed. My Pip's shoulder sensitivity is a classic example of this.

In essence, though, the horse does point the way forward by communicating with us and an understanding of its language is essential, if we wish to understand our equine friends. Unfortunately, it is not quite as simple as some suggest. For example ears back may mean different things in varying contexts. This is a bit like a human's use of the word "good". Does it always mean *good*? What about "Good, let's do it."? Or "Oh, he's good alright" when talking about a warmonger who has just invaded two countries and legitimised torture in his own? Not to mention "When she's bad, she's very good". In a word, context is everything.

Context is no less significant in the way of the horse. Ears back may mean "I am pissed off". Yet it could also mean "I am dozing" or "I am concentrating". Other aspects of the horse's body language and the context of your relationship with your equine friend will provide the clues as to its intended meaning. Nevertheless, if there is a single beacon which can point you in the direction of properly understanding your horse's language of "physiology and movement", it is likely to be the eye. In a nutshell, if it is hard and unyielding, you have a problem but, if it is soft and yielding, you are on target.

To ride or not to ride?
Vicki and I have had numerous discussions – many of them heated – about methods, techniques, devices and the approaches advanced by the gurus we turn to at times for guidance. If I have learned anything from those debates, it is that, while some of those gizmos lend themselves to abuse, it is also possible for someone riding with a bit in the horse's mouth and a saddle on its back to be kinder and more sensitive to their mount than a well-meaning but clueless rider who bounces around on a horse's naked back while clinging to a cordeo wrapped tightly around its upper neck.

Having said this, it has become abundantly clear to me that riding inherently poses a potential danger to the horse's physical and mental well-being. For this reason I believe that any path towards riding must include contemplation of the question, "To ride or not to ride?". The only creature that can answer this question in such a way that we will know that riding is entirely acceptable to our equine friend is neither you nor I but the horse. For this reason I have decided to approach my preparations for riding Pip on this basis: I will not ride her, until and unless she makes it clear that this is entirely acceptable to her. How will I know? The answer will be in her eye.

In this vein I would like to leave you with a lengthy quote from Stormy May, for she says it much better than I can:

> As a person progresses in her understanding of horse language, with its syntax of anatomy, physiology, and psychology, there may come a time when it is appropriate to get on a horse's back. Just as signposts point the way to a destination, I can give a hint about some of the elements that will need to be understood by the person who has endeavoured to learn enough of the horse's language to get to a point where being astride might be a helpful step in her lessons. As a human endeavours to learn the way a horse's body is designed, the way certain muscles, tendons, and ligaments work in concert with the skeletal structure, and the capacities and limits of these physiological elements, he will learn ways to "play" with the horse that lead to more freedom and balance for the horse. In the same way that yoga can help balance our own bodies and spirits, the person will learn the yoga which balances and frees a horse to enable her to greater expression.
>
> The next signpost is when the person learns how to work with the horse with greater discipline, when both human and horse apply themselves to specific elements to develop the physiology of the horse and the mental focus and concentration of both horse and human. Around this time, another signpost you might notice is that the personal desire of the human to ride the horse will have naturally dropped away. A person at this level of understanding would have no more wish to bridle and saddle her equine teacher than she would to bridle and saddle her best human friend and prod her along a nice "trail ride."

If you are at the beginning of this journey and can't quite understand yet how a person could have a fulfilling relationship with a horse without riding, maybe it would be helpful to have a little carrot hung out to tempt you. When a human has learned the horse's language well enough that she begins to dance with her equine partner, she collects and balances him not as the end result of pulling, tugging, and restraining, but as the result of speaking a common language, never causing pain at any point along the path; she simply learns how to dance with his movements as a partner. Only then will the horse's anatomy reveal that he may indeed carry a human as part of the dance, on a strengthened spine that has not been weakened by hours of a rider pounding on the saddle, with muscles that are free from painful pressure sores, carried in a flexed and contracted state which leads to higher blood pressure within the muscle and the ability of this muscle to endure the pressure from a vertical load for a few minutes at a time.

(*Path of the Horse*, p. 35).

To Ride or Not to Ride: Is This Really the Question?
11 May 2014

In my last post I posed the question, To ride or not to ride?, and stated quite emphatically that this was not only the question, but the one all of us who are contemplating riding a horse should seriously ask ourselves before venturing onto the back of a creature whom we claim to love as a good friend. As the debate got underway two things happened which have since caused me to reconsider whether it is indeed the question that we should be asking ourselves. Perhaps there is a more fundamental issue at stake, one which I had ignored. Then Michael Bevilacqua posted his comment and I immediately knew what it was. I would like to deal with that issue now.

So what happened?
First of all, there were the comments themselves, many or most of which, if not all, are profound. In the interests of those of our readers who find time to read the posts but not follow the discussion, I would like to deal with some of the points made, if only because they are so pertinent and valid in the light of the issues at stake.

Secondly, there was Pip. My mare decided to make a comment of her own on my contemplation of the question as to whether I should ride her or not. It was a comment which has been decidedly challenging, enough to warrant a re-examination of the question, *To ride or not to ride?*, to the extent that it caused me to question whether the very question itself was not completely off target. Pip's comment too I would like to share with you.

The science
It is interesting to note that only one of the comments questioned the scientific knowledge that we have at our disposal when it comes to

determining whether riding is hazardous to the horse. Kelly writes the following:

> I used to earn a living by taking young people out hiking in the wilderness. In the course of this full time work I weighed around 58kg and regularly carried back packs in the range of 20-25kg. The packs were carried for long periods of time, day in day out.

> I know I am not a horse, but humans have the same structural make up of cells and blood vessels as horses. So why did I not suffer any pressure damage to my shoulder muscles?

On the face of it this question seems to concern the human shoulders. The context within which it is situated, however, suggests otherwise, for it is introduced as follows: "When the study of the pressure exerted by a saddle and rider are discussed, and how this pressure cuts off capillary blood circulation and starts cellular death in the muscles, the following question arises in me". Put another way, you might restate the question in the light of its context as follows: "If I didn't suffer any pressure damage to my shoulder muscles, how could the pressure exerted by a saddle and rider inflict such injury on a horse?", which is of course as legitimate a question, as the one Kelly actually poses.

Human shoulders and equine backs

As I understand it, a human finds it easiest to carry a load on the shoulders, because it is not merely borne by those body parts but by the entire upright skeletal frame with the exception of the head and neck, albeit that the shoulders and to a lesser but significant extent the back and chest bear the brunt of it. Personally, I would nevertheless be very surprised to hear that any human would not suffer pressure injury to their shoulder muscles when carrying that amount of weight for a prolonged period of time. While I may not be crippled by carrying my lightweight video camera in a small rucksack on my back while on holiday, I definitely notice that I have been carrying it when I remove it. Perhaps this is just another way of asking how much injury do you need to suffer before you experience pain. Of course, once the source of discomfort is permanently removed, the body has a chance to recover and any pain, however slight, becomes a distant memory. If she could speak, Pip might corroborate this based on her experience of two years without being ridden regularly following a history during which she felt pressure on her withers injurious enough to leave vivid scars.

Naturally, a horse's back is very different body part and is designed primarily to carry the abdominal barrel and part of the thoracic cavity, and to transfer the dynamic energy produced by the hindquarters to the forequarters to facilitate movement. Any vet worth their oats will candidly tell you that the horse's back was never designed to carry weight on top of it and that includes the two-legged variety. One of the reasons for this is that, unlike a human's shoulders, an equine back has no support structure below it. In addition, it is proportionately long, which means that it is more susceptible to sagging, much like a long plank serving as a makeshift bridge across a stream. Then there is the fact that, although the forelegs carry the bulk of the horse's weight, their bony structures are not directly connected to the spine. Instead, that weight is carried in a veritable sling of soft tissue (muscles, ligaments, tendons and so forth) supported on either side by the forelegs. By this stage you would be quite right to conclude that human shoulders are proportionately far stronger than equine backs.

Helping the horse support the human
This is also the reason why the two main styles of riding in the equestrian world – "Western" and "classical" or "English" – seek to help the horse support the human by espousing a mode of riding which tries to avoid hollowing the back. Western riding seeks to do this by keeping the head relatively low at the end of a straight neck. This has the effect of stretching (that is, relaxing) the back muscles, while engaging their abdominal counterparts. The classical tradition tries to achieve the same by encouraging the horse to step further under its body, thereby seeking to stretch the back muscles from the hindquarters. At the same time the horse is supposed to raise the

base of its neck thereby shifting its centre of gravity (and hence more of its weight) towards the rear, which would also have the effect of causing the horse to bend its head down at the poll in order to maintain its balance, lengthening the back muscles from the front at the same time. The advantage of the classical tradition is that the weight is spread more evenly over all of the legs rather than predominantly on the forequarters, as is the case with Western riding.

The only way either 'solution" can "work" is if the horse carries itself, as opposed to being "carried" by the rider with the aid of a combination of instruments of force and restraint. In the classical tradition this is what is known as self-collection or self-carriage and what Michael Bevilacqua refers to as "natural collection". It represents a form of movement which is safest – this is not the same as injury-free – for the horse when ridden. Unfortunately, it is also something which is quite rare to find in the classical tradition and virtually impossible at what passes for the summit of equestrian endeavours at the Olympic Games, the World Equestrian Games and other similarly saddening gatherings. You will know it when the instruments of force and restraint are abandoned and you see the horse carry itself. I know of only three public figures who have shown that they are capable of helping a horse do just this: Alexander Nevzorov, Michael Bevilacqua and Klaus Ferdinand Hempfling.

Throwing off the tack
Referring to Alexander Nevzorov, Lina has this to say and it is worth quoting her in full in order to illustrate the point:

> To me it was obvious that the horses in the videos in which he rode with only the cordeo, were the same horses he had used a bridle and bits on previously. I have seen many people who have trained their horses the "traditional" way if you will... with saddles and bridles, be able to work beautifully with their horses bareback and with a halter or just a rope (cordeo) around their neck. They already knew the movements. I can do this to some extent myself with my own trail horses, as can

a few of my fellow trail riders – these are not riders who compete in any way shape or form, or do haute ecole, but simply, they have ridden their horses in saddles and bridles and can then take it all off and the horses know the commands because they come from trust, the seat, the legs, the intention, etc. etc.

It may be true that Alexander Nevzorov trained his horses the traditional way first. It may also be true that Michael Bevilacqua did so as well, as did Hempfling with Ferdinand with that graceful Lipizzaner which dances with him in a video that has garnered more viewings than probably any other YouTube video on the subject. It may also be true that Lina has seen many people "able to work beautifully with their horses bareback and with a halter or just a rope (cordeo) around their neck". The question though is not whether the humans are capable of doing this but whether the horses can carry themselves in natural collection when the tack is thrown off and instruments of force and restraint are abandoned.

A quick search of YouTube will soon reveal that there are very few horses that are capable of carrying themselves in natural collection when the tack is thrown off and they are no longer held together in a frame. This should not be surprising, if one notes that it is possible to score 92.3% at an FEI World Cup Dressage show (the very summit of equestrian prowess, so we are led to believe) on a horse that is not even being ridden in self-collection with all of the tack on! Indeed, for much of the time it is ridden behind the bit (the bit is behind an imaginary vertical line from the poll down), with the crest of the neck as its highest point rather than the poll and hind legs which barely reach underneath the body in trot. Now take away the tack and ask yourself whether the "beauty" of what is not even natural collection will not collapse like a house of cards.

The bottom line

So is riding really detrimental to the horse? Michael Bevilacqua is emphatic: "There is no question about riding a horse being bad for a horse." Yet he used to ride in the past, just as Nevzorov did, albeit only in natural collection and for brief periods at a time, once he had reached a certain level of awareness. In addition, he also quite candidly states the following:

> I still support and encourage people, even if their only major decision, is to use a bitless bridle. 2013 was my last seminar, and, yet, it was like a chapter from the past of NHE (Nevzorov Haute Ecole). Riding was still possible, if only in natural collection.

Jade has also encountered evidence that riding can be physically detrimental to a horse. She proposes a need for further research, contemplation and greater responsibility on the part of riders:

> The first thing that comes to mind is that there needs to be more unbiased scientific research into the effects of riding on the horse. Both short-term and long-term, all kinds of riding styles, tackless vs with tack, durations of ride etc. Another thing to research would be the effects of starting the horse later in life, i.e. when completely mature. And whether this makes a difference when it comes to riding. Hopefully, this would lead to a more responsible approach to riding for people who still think that it is a necessary part of the horse-human relationship.

Some of the science on the effects of riding.

The bottom line is that we already know from the research which has already been conducted that riding not only has the potential to be detrimental to the horse but that it can also inflict permanent injury. Although the mental anguish involved can be extreme, here I would like to confine my comments to the physical. Again, evidence suggests that, while riding in natural collection without instruments of pain for relatively brief periods at a time may place some physical strain on the horse, it is unlikely to cause harm. Having said that, I would again like to note that it is possible for an accomplished rider to ride a horse with a fairly harsh bit in natural collection on a loose rein (which of course begs the question as to why one would use a bit in the first place) while inflicting far less discomfort than someone riding with nothing more than a neck ring (cordeo) hooning around with the horse's head up in the air, its back hollow and the neck rope collected around its throat.

Survival and learned helplessness

So what about Gary's legitimate query:

> Widely respected horsemen such as Mark Rashid, (in spite of his continued use of the bit) show enormous kindness and consideration for the welfare and well-being of their horses. And yet as a "working cowboy" he has spent on many occasions, either working cattle or running a "dude ranch", very long hours in the saddle.......is that an unforgivable way to behave from a man so "in tune" with horses? Do his horses back away in obvious disapproval when he approaches them with a saddle after remembering that "really long ride" yesterday? I think not. I would be interested to know his view on this subject....

I would not wish to comment on Mark Rashid's approach to riding or that of his horses, even if I felt competent to do so, which I do not. Yet I do not believe that his view on the subject is quite as relevant as that of the horse. The urge to survive is instinctive in the horse and its ability to do so is legendary. Domesticated horses employ an array of techniques to survive their humans' attention including flight, fight and learned helplessness. In many, if not most cases they are not aware of a regime of care and riding other than that which they are accustomed to and so they learn to survive it, even if this means shutting down and doing all that is required of them without protest. You will see it in the eye. In extreme cases the light has gone out. The spirit is dead.

Riding is potentially harmful physically but....

Of course, the physical is not the only dimension of the horse. Mental, emotional and some would even argue, spiritual dimensions are also common to the horse. The challenge of being ridden in natural collection for relatively brief periods at a time may demand much the horse physically and perhaps even cause some minor stress. Penka asks:

> At the same time, Olympic Athletes need good Trainers to help them push the limits and challenge the perceptions of what they are capable of? Can this be the case with horses? We probably don't need to be on their backs to do that....

Yet even if we are on their backs when we do that, could it not be that the horse may derive some benefit from such contact with a human within its mental, emotional or spiritual dimension? Perhaps this is what Geerteke is suggesting when she writes the following:

> What if "riding" is part of horse's wish to become aware? What if by denying horse's wish to be ridden human denies horse to evolve? Would that in the core not be an equally cruel act as riding a horse that does NOT wish to be ridden?

> And would it not be almost a natural consequence that disease occurring in human when not listening to its inner voice will also occur in horse when horse is not being listened to its inner voice?

Is this bullshit or is there an element of truth to it?

These questions are challenging especially when viewed within the context of the relationship between horses and humans over the centuries. The species have gravitated towards each other in a symbiosis which has encompassed so many different spheres of interaction, including culture, work, sport, religion, health care and entertainment to mention a few. Those who have attended courses with Klaus Ferdinand Hempfling will be aware of the idea of a horse and a human complementing each other to produce a transfigured entity – most visibly expressed in the horse bearing the human – whose combined power and beauty are greater than the sum of its parts. Nowadays horses depend upon humans for their very survival, even in the wild. Conversely though, a growing number of humans are beginning to discover that, if they are to survive as humans and not merely as blighted parodies of the species, horses have much to teach them. Perhaps riding may to some extent constitute part of the process whereby horses and humans derive benefits from each other which extend beyond the physical dimension.

Doubts

To ride or not to ride? The question is challenging if you are open to asking it. Many of us would like to ride but we have doubts about whether we should. Here are a few which some of our readers have expressed.

Penka:

> I also think that we do it with good intentions and we feel that we have fulfilling relationships with our horses. They are probably ("definitely") more fulfilling for us then for the horse and deep down we know that the feeling can be better if truly reciprocated... Yet, is this any worse than the parent projecting his ideas or life principles on the child? The rationale is obvious – good intentions, no major harm, should help, I know it better...

I know someone who feels it is okay to use a little bit of force with her horse, if your intentions are honourable, for instance, if you have just mounted your horse but it does not want to move forward. A tug or a smack accompanied by verbal encouragement such as "Come on. Let's go. Now!", much as you might do with a small child (so I am told, which I have to rely on, as I have never had one of my own). My response takes the form of a question: Why should the horse have to move forward with you on its back (or whatever else you are trying to force the horse to do)? Indeed, what gives a human the right to force a horse to do anything? Having said that, there are moments when one simply has to urge a horse to do something, for instance if its health and well-being depend on it. My experience though is that a horse tends to pick up on urgency in the energy one radiates and then responds accordingly, especially if it is a horse with whom you have a close relationship.

Susan:

> I am thankful to all those who have alerted us to the physical consequences of being careless and uncaring about our horses' backs and bodies, and as a result of their research I now ride less frequently and for much shorter periods, and do

a lot of ground work and play and gymnasticising to help my horse feel fitter and more supple, just like yoga helps my not-so-young body, so that his energy and enthusiasm might meet with mine and give us the pleasure of going out and about together without my feeling the compulsion to push him or force him where no horse would willingly care to go....

Noble sentiments, yet Susan immediately questions them: "Is this a cop-out on my part? Am I kidding myself just the same way as those who believe in rollkur are able to kid themselves that 'it's OK'?" Why question them?

Gary:

My feeling (OK my imaginative speculation) is that it often comes down to the specific combination of horse and rider and were it possible to interview all horses on the subject there would be just as many who said they enjoyed carrying their rider and felt no ill effects as there would be horses complaining about a sore back and associated ailments. Yes, it could be just wishful thinking on my part as on balance I would like to ride. For the moment as you can gather from this comment, I am sitting on the fence....

I read this and thought: this is as honest as it gets.

Something also niggled me when I read these comments. To ride or not to ride? Is this really the question?

So which way to go?

To ride or not to ride? If this is the question, what should we do? Which way should we go? Three people came up with an answer which renders the horse's response paramount, albeit inevitably only through the human's interpretation of that response.

Jade:

The second thing that comes to mind is that, although this can be an extensive and difficult topic, the basis of it is very simple. Go and ask your equine partner. In the end, it's always going to be about the relationship and doing what works for the individual horse-human partnership.

Glenn:

> The TRONTR [To Ride or Not to Ride] question has been on my mind for a while and a few years back I wrote this: http://www.waterfallcreek.com.au/Open-Attachment/51/ The%20Big%20Question%20PDF.pdf. Simple question with no clear cut answer apart from listening to one's inner, intuitive voice, and knowing your horse.

> Now I would add, "Listen to your horse, and yourself, and if all is good then get on with it".

Kelly:

> The other day, in my mind, Jasper showed me clearly that he was ok with it all. He walked at liberty with me out of the paddock and away from his herd of 12 horses, he walked with me across the front lawn and loaded at liberty onto the truck. Whenever we load up on the truck the simple fact is that we are going riding. I am not trying to justify whether it is right or wrong to ride, each person will find their own way with this and come to their own conclusion, but I am saying – let us not beat ourselves up too much about it all. There are many shades of grey, and only you and your horse will know what is right or wrong in that moment.

Pip's comment

While I was working on my last post, something happened which caused me to doubt part of what I had written. For some weeks I had been working with her to help her prepare her body for the time when I felt it would be alright to pop the question: To ride or not to ride? Would she allow me? As usual, I tried to vary our activities, yet always seemed to be focusing on the goal of riding.

Then Pip commented. Initially, I did not hear her. Pip is not like Anaïs. When Vicki's mare comments, she raises herself majestically upright like a totem pole to impress upon one the folly of messing with close to 600 kg of perpendicular horse. It is impossible not to hear Anaïs when she comments. I tend to listen very quickly. More importantly, I have become very adept at avoiding situations when she may feel a need to comment.

Pip, on the other hand, is the introspective type. She turns inward and closes down communication. In the early days of our relationship I thought that Anaïs was the more difficult horse to deal with but she is not. In fact, she is a big pussy cat. Because she is so expressive, it is much easier to find a way to ensure that those big brown eyes remain soft as butter. Shutting me out, Pip makes far greater demands of me and I have to dig very deep to re-establish contact with her.

So what was Pip's comment. As I understand it, she was telling me that I had become so focused on this question of riding, that the bossy little man within me had become so insistent on his riding agenda that he was beginning to lose sight of the horse in front of him and the relationship that he wants with that horse. I was ashamed.

A break

Fortunately, a break had been planned. Vicki and I managed to find cheap tickets to the Algarve in southern Portugal (I just love the language, although I can only understand one word of it: *obrigado* – thank you), so we headed there to celebrate my birthday. It is a lovely part of the world with relatively few people, except during the summer when the population triples.

The break created the distance from Pip and the demands of work which I needed to assess what I had been doing with my horse and to re-evaluate my relationship with her. To ride or not to ride? Is it indeed the question? Or was there not something more important at stake? Upon our return to Holland, I felt the answer. I knew and know what kind of human I want to be with Pip and, if that means that riding may be ruled out, so be it. And the moment I let go of the question of to ride or not, Pip and I started to have fun again and we celebrated her birthday soon after our return, reconnected once more.

No, I have not abandoned the prospect of Pip allowing me to ride. We are still doing exercises together which help her to carry herself but the goal of riding no longer dictates the nature of my interaction with Pip. If I ever ride her, this will occur as something incidental to the essence of our mutual enjoyment of each other's company.

The question has to do with the human, not the horse
A little over a week after our return from the Algarve, Michael Bevilacqua's comment arrived. I read it and then reread it the next day. Suddenly I knew how to formulate what I had come to feel intuitively with Pip. This quote from Michael helped:

> There is no question about riding a horse being bad for a horse. However, the question remains about riding – and, subsequently, it has nothing to do with the horse but the people.

We may be tempted to say that we should ask our horse if it is okay to get on its back. It is a temptation that I think we should yield to with great commitment. Yet we should perhaps be aware that the answer is ultimately going to depend upon our interpretation. Ultimately, it is the human who mounts the horse's back and not the horse that mounts the human on its back. Put another way, the question of to ride or not to ride has nothing to do with the horse but the human and, as such, the answer is ultimately our responsibility.

Is it not about love?
But there was more. Michael Bevilacqua wrote something which left me feeling puzzled enough to chew on and chomp over for several days:

> I made a tacky, home-made video to go along with my book that was like a "special features" video along with movies. In it, I did say that, sometimes, *trying to explain this to people was like trying to explain how to love*. [Emphasis added.]

I looked at this and kept asking myself the question, "Trying to explain *this*": What is *this*? What does he mean when he refers to *this*. Then I had an epiphany and the light came on. What has Michael Bevilacqua been trying to explain to people? Not only have I read his book several times and his articles too but I have also attended one of his seminars. *This* must refer to everything that he has been trying to explain in his publications and public events. And what was he trying to explain? How to love!

The real question

Trite? No. Profound? Absolutely! There are so many humans looking for a dream horse and a beautiful relationship with that product of their dreams. How? This is what we ask. How can we develop a beautiful relationship with our dream horse? In his book, appropriately entitled *Beyond the Dream Horse*, Michael Bevilacqua provides the answer, just as he has been doing in all of his work with horses and humans. Love. Simply love your horse! It is the beginning of everything.

Which led me to re-examine the question: To ride or not to ride? For far too long we humans have subconsciously been basing our entire relationship with horses on this question and the answer we almost inevitably come up with: ride. We have reduced our relationship with our so-called equine friends to the interface of the horse's back and the human's bum and almost all we do in relation to the horse is mediated by that interface. Perhaps it is time to replace the question, *To ride or not to ride?* with something else. Perhaps we need to move away from back and bum to horse and human. Is not the real question simply, "Do I love my horse?" and, if it is and my reply is "Yes!", then should I not simply go and love my horse and let all that we do together, horse and human, follow from that love, including the decision as to whether to ride or not?

Tales of love

Alexia's pen is poignant:

> Once one's eyes are opened they can never be closed again in ignorance and it seems doors have shut to some of what I thought were "simple" joys.

Ah, but have they shut? And if some have, have not others opened? I do not believe that I or anyone else can dictate whether a human should ride a horse or not. I do believe, however, that riding may be possible in my relationship with Pip. Yet the story that I wish to write with Pip is not of riding but of love and, if she allows me on her back, it will follow from that love.

In the meantime I would like to leave you with these tales of love contributed by two or our readers. I melted in humility when I read them, tales of love from the old and the young.

Peggy:

> Firefly my Brumby pony is not likely to ever be ridden, while she is in my care, yet we have a great time playing Games at Liberty . Sunny my Q.H. gelding has never been ridden for years, I took him on as basically a rescue horse that had foundered badly, & has a leg problem, but at times loves to do something just to show me he can do simple ground game at the walk, like the others. (His choice entirely) Now Cracker my "Riding Horse" also does great liberty Groundwork ....Plus Ridden Games with the ball, tarps, cavalletti, bending poles and anything else I can find to make his ride/play interesting. We have been riding with only a neck string lately in my arena, when we go out on a trail ride I walk with him for at least ten minutes, then mount on a log in the bush. I ride him out in a halter and we just wander about the beautiful bush tracks. (Just the two of us)...........So it is Riding!!!!!!........But NOT.. No Nonsense Stuff without consideration for the animal that so many have to endure.... "I Trust Him With My Life"........I believe the rides on Cracker are as pleasurable for him as it is for me, and he gets a lovely extra feed for his consideration & time with me...

> Every morning I Meditate in my stable and my Horses are free to join me & they usually do,......... followed by Energy Healing with them. With heads low, yawning, licking & chewing eyes closed etc. I get my hands, arms & legs licked, hair groomed gently, a gentle nose resting on my shoulder or back or a horse cheek against my face. ....My horses know how much I love & cherish them...

Jade:

> Cisco and I decided a while ago that riding is not something either of us find enjoyable to do together. So it is something

we will never do. Dougie is only just three, so I will not present the concept of riding to him for a few years yet. Maybe when he is seven or eight, I will ask how he feels about it. It will be up to him. For now we have so many other activities to explore together....

P.S.

Michael Bevilacqua writes of me and others: "It still surprises me that he, and others, differentiate me from NHE. I find that it is the same message." I draw a distinction between Michael, on the one hand, and Nevzorov and Nevzorov Haute Ecole, on the other, in as much as I see a difference between his non-judgmental, inclusive approach and theirs. While I am aware that Cloé Lacroix, the dean of the NHE school and Michael's friend and colleague, is sincerely trying to make the school more inclusive and Lydia Nevzorova and the NHE press are producing a growing number of horse-friendly publications in their efforts to make the world a better place for horses, it is difficult for NHE to shake off its history of intolerance of other approaches towards achieving the same goal.

A message is more than just its substance. It also includes the form in which it is packaged and expressed. To my knowledge (please correct me if I am wrong), NHE is still as intolerant of other trainers as Klaus Ferdinand Hempfling and Chuck Mintzlaff have previously shown themselves to be. In addition, NHE relies to a large extent on the publications of Alexander Nevzorov, a number of which read as vivid examples of the art of vilification employing the most acerbic, if not barbed, wit and rhetorical devices couched in irony and dripping with sarcasm.

Michael Bevilacqua, on the other hand, includes and encourages people in word and deed, eschewing judgment and condemnation. The difference, as I see it, is immense.

Two Spirits, One Human and the Horse
9 June 2014

Standing in front of the noble head, the arching neck, the muscled shoulders and graceful legs of the horse, a human is asked a single profound question each and every time: Who are you? Are you two spirits: the one whom I sense you are and the one whom you claim to be? Or are those spirits one? Is there congruence between yourself and your sense of self? Or is there a gap between the two so wide that I can put my hoof through it? Who are you? When you stand before the horse, can you answer that question as unambiguously and truthfully as the creature before you can? And if there are two spirits when the horse expects only one, what do you do to unite them in the single human whom you are?

Two spirits
The notion of two spirits is derived from native American culture, in which it denoted what is potentially one of the most extreme forms of alienation between self and sense of self, where each is located within a different gender identity. A human might have a male body (their external identity) but a female consciousness (their internal identity) or vice versa, a situation which manifests itself in transgender behaviour.

Perhaps the most obvious example of such transgender behaviour in contemporary Western society is where a human with a male body but a female sense of self adopts feminine mannerisms and dresses in women's clothing. Taken to its logical conclusion, the human may even undergo hormone therapy and reconstructive surgery to remove the external vestiges of their sex and attempt to replicate female bodily characteristics. Although perhaps less obvious, there are also numerous cases of humans in a female body who seek to do the opposite.

Transgender

Humans may express their gender identity in a variety of forms in between these extremes (from male to female and vice versa). For the sake of convenience we refer to this as transgender behaviour. Essentially it merely refers to a situation in which a human's sense of self does not strictly conform to society's general expectations in relation to the biological sex assigned to them at birth.

Returning to the terminology of indigenous American culture, two-spirit humans are not peculiar to that or Western culture. They may be found in a multiplicity of cultures right around the world from the Americas to Asia, where their existence is recorded in numerous countries including China, Japan and India. Earlier this year the Supreme Court of India even went so far as to recognise the existence of transgender as a third gender in order to uphold human rights. To this extent, although they may not be as numerous as their "straight" heterosexual human cousins, the presence of transgender individual around the globe is by no means extraordinary.

From saint to singer

Neither is the transgender phenomenon merely a modern "aberration", as some would have us believe. Not only are there documented instances of transgender humans featuring in history but some have even attained highly popular status. Even the great religions of the world have not been immune to their presence. Saint Wilgefortis, a bearded woman frequently depicted on a crucifix, was a saint venerated by popular imagination in the Middle Ages to such an extent that she inspired the growth of a sect which spread throughout Europe and a statue of her on a cross may still be viewed in the diocesan museum of Graz in Austria.

Perhaps it should therefore come as no surprise to greet the resurrection of the bearded lady from Austria seven centuries later. This year the Eurovision Song Contest, one of the most popular music shows in the world, was won by Conchita Wurst, the "female" alter ego of the bearded performer, Tom Neuwirth, a 25-year-old male who describes himself as gay and who moved to Graz in his teens to study fashion design. Little imagination is required to guess the source of his – or should it be *her* – inspiration. Like the medieval forerunner of Mr Neuwirth, aka Ms Wurst, the twenty-first century's bearded lady proved to be exceptionally popular throughout Europe, winning the Eurovision Song Contest with a spectacular margin from the runners-up from the Netherlands.

So what?

So what has this got to do with the horse? Like death, the horse is a great leveller. Whether you are as powerful as the reincarnation of Napoleon astride his white horse, as successful an equestrian as the Dutch dressage rider, Anky van Grunsven, as straight in your gender preferences as Vladimir Putin or as bent as Conchita Wurst, or as socially insignificant as you and I, when you stand before the horse, you are still only asked one question: Are you the authentic you?

Ultimately, to the horse the appearance of the human before it is entirely secondary to the nature of that human. Are you two spirits: the one whom the horse senses you are and the one whom you claim to be? Or are those spirits one? Is there congruence between yourself and your sense of self? Or is there a gap between the two so wide that the horse can put its hoof through it? Who are you?

Jasmijn

There is a human whom I know, respect and admire, because of who they are, what they have experienced, the journey they are embarked upon, and their prowess and sensitivity with the horse. Although I had been familiar with their story for some time before, the first personal contact I personally had with that human occurred in the form of a photograph sent to me from their mobile phone within hours of fleeing Klaus Ferdinand Hempfling's one-year school on 20 July 2012.

At the time I knew that human as Jasmijn, a young woman who felt an urgent need to abandon the master whose work with horses she so admired and her dream of becoming a Klaus Ferdinand

Hempfling body awareness and horse practitioner, a prospect which the master who dances with horses had held out to her and her fellow students in return for a truckload of cash. And I wondered at the amount of pressure she must have felt she was under at the hands of her remaining fellow students (with the exception of the only other young student) and her teacher to have abandoned so much, including the prospect of losing the remainder of her fee.

Jason

Today I know that same human as Jason, a young man who feels so ill at ease in the body into which he was born, that he has decided to do something about it. He has embarked upon what is perhaps the most challenging journey of his life to become the man whom he knows he should be. This is the same human whom I respected and admired as Jasmijn, and whom I now respect and admire as Jason.

Since Jasmijn has embarked upon the transition to Jason, I have seen him at play with horses and again I have been so impressed by what I first saw when she danced with her young stallion, Eno del Cid, before Vicki and myself in Belgium in 2012. Only this time I detect a major difference. Jason is far more self-assured than the Jasmijn of the past but without having lost that fine sensitivity and alertness to the horse before him. As the pressures grow to become a man – and as a man I can tell you that there are many – it is my fondest wish that Jason never lose such sensitivity.

The same human

When Jason is before the horse, he is asked the same question that he was asked when he was still Jasmijn, the same that all of us are asked when we stand before the noble head, the arching neck, the muscled shoulders and graceful legs of the horse. Who are you? Are your two spirits one? Judging from the response of the horse, as I saw then and see now, Jason's answer is essentially the same, only this time he is able to answer the question more emphatically: whether my hair is long and girlish in a ponytail or short and boyish in a cropped style, I am my authentic self.

Jason Alexander Wauters is the same human who can boast the extraordinary achievements of Jasmijn Wauters in their relations with horses:

- he studied Hempfling's approach towards horses through the latter's books and videos;
- he attended Hempfling's Pure Practical Performance course in 2010;
- during the period from September 2011 to July 2012 he spent a total of a little over seven and a half months attending a full-time course with Hempfling along with nine other students, a course which finally ended after two years with only seven students left;
- during his studies with Hempfling he worked with three different stallions, which he had taken with him to Hempfling's school;
- he was the only student who regularly worked with a stallion during his studies with Hempfling;
- he was only one of two of the one-year students whom Hempfling felt were good enough to feature briefly in one of the numerous videos featuring the one-year course, which he published on YouTube;
- he is the only one-year student whom Hempfling felt was good enough to show training a horse in one of his YouTube videos;
- he is the founder of EDEN – Escuela del Equilibrio Natural, a successful school dedicated to helping humans and their horses find each other.

Next month Jason will be starting a programme of lessons and activities with Pip and myself in an effort to help my mare and I bridge the last gaps that separate us, especially when she is at liberty and is required to find her own physical, mental, emotional and spiritual balance. I hope to share that experience with you in this blog.

Towards Riding 3 – Taking Stock and Equine Touch
6 July 2014

As I contemplate riding Pip and the preparations required for this, I feel a pressing need to take stock of our achievements – my mare's but predominantly mine – and to reassess the direction in which I am travelling in order to clarify the "big picture" within which these preparations are occurring and to adjust course if necessary. This has partly been prompted by the achievement of a major milestone in my studies of horses and ways of helping them and their carers. While we are all probably aware of the importance of taking stock in theory, actually doing it again has been very educational. So how has this affected Pip, me and my perception of the point we are at?

Pip
Let us start by taking stock of my preparations to ride my favourite horse. I had originally hoped to be riding her by now but first I had to contend with my failing her by focusing on the goal at the expense of our relationship as outlined in my post entitled *To Ride or Not to Ride: Is This Really the Question?*

Then there is the issue of her back, which Jason Wauters has described as sensitive. Vicki and I have both noticed that she seems to be stiff in the sacrum. There seems to be little movement around the lumbar area pelvic region, which makes it difficult for Pip to step under. This is probably mainly due to the fact that she was ridden skew for so many years. As a result she is reluctant to canter on the circle. I am inclined to devote more attention to this issue before venturing onto her back.

In my last straightness training lesson I also discovered that I have a major difference in approach with my instructor. It would appear that the model of pressure and release, which is so prevalent in horse training circles, is a very difficult one to let go of.

Essentially, this approach requires the application of pressure to the horse until it yields to that pressure and responds as required, at which point it is rewarded with a release of that pressure. As such, it is a form of negative reinforcement, which research has shown to be a highly inefficient form of training compared to positive reinforcement.

Another shortcoming of this approach lies in the fact that, where the pressure is physical (that is, force), a horse's natural response is to resist such pressure and not yield to it. More fundamentally, the application of pressure assumes the existence of compulsion, which is to say, the human compels the horse to do something. My question is whether such an approach is commensurate with the type of relationship which I want with Pip, namely, one based on my love and her trust, one in which she is a willing partner and not a yielding servant. This is not to say that I get it right all the time. I do not and Vicki can testify to this. What is does mean is that the guiding principle of our relationship (and hence also our training) must be appropriate.

Equine Touch

The milestone which I refer to above is the completion of my Equine Touch studies for the purposes of becoming a practitioner. From the time Vicki and I got back from our last Equine Touch course in England at the beginning of February until the end of May, each of us performed a total in excess of sixty Equine Touch sessions on more than twenty different horses. We were then required to compile detailed reports on the sessions involving each horse along with pictures and diagrams.

In addition, we had to complete written assignments on Equine Touch theory, and the anatomy and physiology of the horse. Towards the end of May we realised just how much work was involved and shut our business for about ten days to clear the workload. To give you some idea of what was involved, I produced answers totalling 16,000 words, while Vicki managed 26,000 words (that is the equivalent of half a novel). Once that was all done, we still had an essay of no less than 2000 words to write. If anyone still has comments about just how easy it is to obtain an equine bodywork practitioner's certificate, you really do not want to speak to me.

Another Equine Touch course

The reason for the rush to complete our studies lay in the fact that we needed to do so, if we wanted to attend a three-day Level 4 course with Ivana Ruddock, a vet and co-founder of the Equine Touch modality, in June. Although this course is not a requirement to become a practitioner, it is mandatory if one wants to stay up-to-date with the latest developments in this modality. As in the case of any discipline, true learning is an ongoing process and Level 4 is designed to introduce practitioners to the latest developments in Equine Touch.

Perhaps Ivana's greatest strength is that she is capable of taking her knowledge of equine veterinary science gleaned not only from years of study but also regular dissections of horses, to help us understand how the various components of soft tissue (muscles, fascia, tendons and ligaments) work together and with the skeletal frame. Coupled with an awareness of equine biomechanics, this knowledge makes it possible for an Equine Touch practitioner to determine the most appropriate course of action when required. Personally, I also came away feeling rather excited, not only because of everything that I had learned about, more in particular, because I now have several more Equine Touch procedures, which I have good reason to believe are going to be highly beneficial for Pip.

Equine Touch conference

Immediately after the Level 4 course Vicki and I attended the ninth annual conference of the International Equine Touch Association (United Kingdom and Ireland), a two-day event held close to the venue for the Level 4 course in the vicinity of Newcastle-upon-Tyne. Attended by numerous Equine Touch instructors and practitioners, mainly from the United Kingdom, but also a sprinkling from Ireland, the Netherlands and Germany, the conference represented a particularly useful way of meeting the wider Equine Touch community and staying abreast of developments affecting horses.

In addition to the Equine Touch component, the conference also featured an array of guest speakers talking about subjects as varied as horses in the care of the RSPCA, equestrian sport, the use of horses in the police force, animal communication, equine dentistry and myofascial release. It was rather distressing to hear the impact which the economic crisis has had on horses and their carers (about 75 cruelty cases in England some ten years ago compared with in excess of 850 now, many of which involved abandoned horses).

At the risk of being critical

I must confess to having some difficulty listening to presentations on equestrian sports and the use of horses in the police force without any discussion of the ethical issues involved. The two speakers dealing with these issues were quite blunt in their assessment to the effect that what they make horses do is highly stressful. In one case we were informed that an eventing horse had torn its deep digital flexor tendon in one of its hind legs. Although it has now healed, all of the experts that had been consulted warned that it is likely to "go again" at any time. After informing us of this, the speaker then went on to assure us that the horse is still being ridden for competition purposes. Yes, the horse does receive Equine Touch but is it likely to be more effective in mitigating the risk of a re-occurrence of that injury, as – to paraphrase a Dutch proverb – me mopping up water while the tap is running? I was also left with the following question: what is in it for the horse?

What I greatly appreciated about the content of the conference, probably more than anything else, was Ivana Ruddock's advice on when to break the rules in one's approach to Equine Touch and her session on Lessons from Anatomy. If I have a wish list for a future conference, it would be to address what I came away with as the greatest need I currently experience, namely, for a thorough understanding of equine biomechanics.

Another Equine Touch course

Immediately after the conference Vicki and I attended a day-long equine mobilisation and stretching course. We learned how to help the horse mobilise its joints and stretch its muscles both passively and actively. Passive stretching involves the human stretching the horse's muscles by bending and extending the limbs, while active stretching sees the human encourage the horse to stretch its own muscles with the aid of positive reinforcement. According to our instructors, research has revealed that consistent stretching exercises can help the horse increase the length and mass of its muscles to a significant extent.

We were very fortunate to have two Equine Touch instructors for the price of one. Emma Overend and Chris Wyllie impressed me greatly with their power of observation, knowledge of anatomy, physiology and biomechanics, and commitment to the well-being of the horse. I came away with the feeling that some of the procedures which I had learned, were going to be of tremendous benefit to Pip as we prepared for riding. Chris also opened her home to us after the course, where we enjoyed drinks and snacks before heading off to spend our remaining day in England playing tourist.

Playing tourist

My limited experience of English weather leaves me with no doubt as to why the English are capable of producing Monty Python and other instances of outlandish and oddball humour. The weather would drive you completely wacky if you did not. Alternatively, perhaps the weather has driven them so wacky that they do. What a surprise then for us to spend close to ten days in England with only one brief sprinkling of rain. This must be some type of record. Martin and Sheila, our kind hosts who opened up their home for us and fed me beer and whisky when I joined them to watch the odd World Cup football match, told us that the north-east gets more sunshine than any other part of the country, an information byte that

I thought odd, given that we were just a short way from the Scottish border.

Whatever the case, Vicki and I spent some time during our visit playing tourist indoors and outdoors together with other conference-goers from the Continent. Being England, castles and pubs were high on the list, although we also got to see some lovely countryside and public gardens. One thing I cannot understand about the English is that with so many horses in the country, they have so few bridle paths in the countryside, which means that hacking is largely confined to public roads, which can be a hazardous business, given the absence of shoulders alongside the tarmac and the locals' penchant for growing hedges along the verge. The absence of bridle paths was rather reminiscent of Australia. In this respect we are particularly fortunate in the Netherlands. It may be a tiny country but bridle paths are to be found almost everywhere outside the urban areas.

Lesson with Jason Alexander Wauters
28 July 2014

Last week Pip and I had our first lesson with Jason Alexander Wauters, the most successful student to emerge from Klaus Ferdinand Hempfling's one-year schooling programme, the only full one-year course he has ever given to date (yes, the same one Vicki and I were originally scheduled to attend). Since then I have had a couple of homework sessions with Pip and I have to say that I am utterly impressed. I would like to share a few of my insights with you here. In addition, I am rounding off this post with recommendations for where you might want to be heading in September if you are really committed to developing a loving relationship with your horse, and would like to share your experiences and learn with other likeminded humans.

Grounding
Jason started the lesson very much as I had hoped he would: with the human rather than the horse. Our first step was to ground (or centre) ourselves. In descriptive terms it took the following form:
1. spread your feet apart to a distance roughly equivalent to the width of your shoulders;
2. ensure that you are breathing comfortably, to which I would add that you should not try and fill or empty your lungs completely and you may want to try and breathe through your belly (this will lower your centre of gravity to your core and give you greater stability and better balance);
3. be aware of your body and your surroundings, and maintain this awareness throughout all the remaining steps;
4. direct your gaze at the horizon but do not focus on a single object;

5. keep a spring in your stance by ensuring that you do not lock your knees;
6. while holding your body straight but relaxed, gently tip yourself forward and backward a few times before finding a comfortable position a little behind the most forward point;
7. now tilt the base of your pelvis backward and forward gently a few time before ending with it tilted forward (what really helps is to swivel your pelvis in a rising arc when you come forward);
8. hold your hands slightly in front of you at waist height and move your fingers slowly as though your are playing an invisible piano;
9. gently swivel your shoulders backwards and forwards a few times to loosen them;
10. starting with your head, slowly lower your upper body while allowing your arms to hang loosely until your hands are a little way above the ground;
11. sway your arms gently to the left and right and backward and forward, always ensuring that they are hanging loosely;
12. raise your body slowly but do it as though you are unfolding your body from the waist up, your head remaining bowed until the rest is upright;
13. find your stance again (where you ended up in Step 5), tilt your pelvis forward and lower your chin to ensure that your head is straight and not directed up or down.

If you have done this correctly, you should end up in a position which resembles how you would sit on a horse with all your energy focused in your core (in your abdomen about a hand's width below your belly button) and your upper body entirely relaxed. More importantly, you will be aware of nothing but your body and your immediate surroundings. In a word, you will experience a sense of well-being and will be in the moment, baggage-free and ready for your horse, which is where Vicki and I ended up. This is a somewhat more extensive version of the one-minute grounding exercise which

I demonstrated during my presentation at the inaugural Corroboree Equus in Australia in September last year. It is an excellent way of preparing for any interaction with your horse and works even better if you regularly perform holistic (involving the physical, mental, emotional and spiritual dimensions), meditative exercises, such as Tai Chi, Feldenkrais or Hempfling's body awareness routines.

It is all about energy

Working, playing, loving, crying and laughing with horses, in fact everything we do with these supremely sensitive beings is ultimately all about energy and the way we guide our own and interact with that of those creatures. Many of us may have been aware of this essential nature of interaction with horses for some time but how many of us have actually come to incorporate this awareness into our everyday relations with our horse?

While reflecting on the grounding exercise which we did with Jason, it occurred to me that what we are essentially trying to achieve when we are with horses (or anywhere else for that matter) is not merely to be but to *be being*. What I mean is that all too often when we do anything, there is a dislocation between our awareness of self and what we are actually doing: the human does something. What we are seeking to achieve is to actually become what we are doing: the human is what the human does. Energy is also constantly in motion even when our minds and bodies are at rest. As such, the essence of being in the moment is precisely that: *being* (as opposed to *be*).

Introspective Pip

As I have frequently mentioned in this blog, Pip is introspective by nature and her escape route from anything she perceives to be threatening takes her inside herself. Her "evasion" sees her close all avenues of communication and shut off, which, when she is moving, takes the form of autopilot often coupled with increased speed. In many posts I have also referred to her tendency to shut down during liberty work or on a long lunge. The closer we are while connected through a lead, the more reassured she is and the better the contact we have, although this is beginning to change.

In this respect it was interesting to note the difference between Pip and Anaïs in the picadero (a square manège of anything from 12 to 15 metres in width often simply demarcated with nothing more than surveyor's tape). Whereas Anaïs is inclined to approach any human who enters the picadero while she is standing in it, Pip has a tendency to look away and wait to see what will happen next. And if she feels it is threatening, she will shut down, even if she has to move out of the way.

Breaking through

The key to helping a horse communicate with us for the purposes of any training, as I interpret what Jason explained to me, is to sensitise the animal to our presence. Conversely, if a horse approaches the human close enough to be uncomfortable, as Anaïs tends to do, we should keep her out of our personal space. This is particularly important with a horse such as Anaïs, as she is quite capable of walking straight through an unsuspecting human's space.

So what should we do with a horse that does not approach the human, as in Pip's case? The first step, according to my interpretation of Jason, was to make Pip aware of my presence as a *dominant* (not a *dominating*) creature in the sense that, although I love her and am committed to her safety and well-being, I am her guide and she needs to know this. So how do I do this in a non-threatening manner? Shaking a strange object (in this case a plastic feed bag) determinedly, simply move through the picadero from one random corner to another, always ensuring that, while being acutely aware of your horse, you do not look at her, and that you are close enough for the horse to want to move away from your path but far enough away not to be viewed as a threat pursuing her.

The idea is not to desensitise Pip, because we want her to remain a horse and not become a robot (which she becomes when she goes on autopilot, a condition which Jason ascribes to traditional lungeing during the many years that she was required to perform dressage up to a fairly high level in the past). In fact we are seeking to sensitise her. This we do through horse-neutral interaction to start off with. This is to say that the human's action is not directed at the horse, although it may have an impact on her. Initially, Pip ignored the mad human moving determinedly from one part of the picadero to the other (me), then skipped out of his path with mild alarm to face away again, and then started to monitor the human and try and anticipate him. We were breaking through.

The first contact
In some cases it may be necessary to follow up the previous exercise by occupying the horse's space, again without focusing on the horse. What the horse does in response to having its space occupied is the horse's responsibility. An exercise such as this would be too much for Pip. This I know from experience (long past thankfully), one which I deeply regret. Jason realised this immediately as well. There was also no need for it, because Pip had responded well.

We were now ready for me to initiate contact with Pip. The idea was for me to approach Pip with the bag in front of me and to gently raise it to ask her to walk forward and then almost immediately to raise it again to ask for her to trot. As soon as she started to trot I was to lower the bag, step backwards and invite Pip to come to me, stop her outside my dynamic sphere and then reward her with a treat. Under Jason's guidance I did this a few times but each time Pip merely stopped and refused to come to me. However, she did keep her eyes on me. This was enough to merit a reward. And that was enough for the first lesson.

Homework
My homework is to practise what we did during the lesson until our next one on Friday (an interval of a fortnight). All that is required is a few minutes every second or third day. As such, it becomes just another way in which Pip and I interact with each other.

And what is Pip doing during our homework sessions? I could not believe it. From the very first practice session, every time I popped her into trot and then stopped to invite her to cross the few metres between us and come to me, she did, as though it was the most normal thing in the world, which is what we want it to be, of course.

Love, trust and guidance

At the end of it all, everything hinges around love, trust and guidance (a bit similar to what Hempfling means when he uses the term, "dominance"). I love Pip and she trusts me to be a guide who will care for and help her. Without this type of relationship, any form of training will never move beyond the mechanical no matter how refined. There will be a human who *is* and who *does* but not one who is *being*, that is authentic. And the horse will know the difference.

Looking back on our first lesson with Jason Alexander Wauters, I see the essence of Hempfling's approach redefined with a depth of sensitivity and joy (and a refreshing absence of ego), which I believe may help Pip and I bridge the last huge gap dividing us, namely her tendency to shut down during liberty work. I also have reason to believe that it will help her to continue to develop her growing self-confidence. Pip will hopefully learn to trust a bit more, not just me but herself as well.

An Evening with Frédéric Pignon
14 August 2014

Twice in the past few years Vicki and I have been booked to travel to France to see Frédéric Pignon in action with horses. On both occasions we were scheduled to fence-sit during a liberty training clinic and we had to cancel each, the first time because Anaïs came down with colic and the second time because the Ice Queen threw us out of her livery yard (along with all of the other remaining paying customers) and we were hard put to find alternative accommodation. Third time lucky they say, and the saying was proved right when we had the opportunity to travel to the Provence in France to see Frédéric Pignon in action in the new Eqi Cheval Libre show which he and his wife Magalí Delgado, have produced. And thanks to a new-found friend and a thunderstorm, I also had a chance to chat to him at the end of it all.

Avignon
The show was scheduled to be staged just outside Monteux, a small town in Vaucluse. Avignon is the nearest city and offered more affordable accommodation than closer to the venue, so we opted to set up base there.

As some of you may be aware, Avignon once served as the seat of the Roman Catholic Church, when six French popes chose to establish their headquarters there during the fourteenth century. Being supremely focused on all things spiritual, these popes also found time and money to erect a truly massive Palais des Papes (literally, Popes' Palace) which yours truly, being a former son of the church, simply had to visit. Fortunately, the French Revolution restored this ostentatious display of earthly pursuits to the people, with the result that it is on display for all to admire or criticise.

For the rest, the city does not boast much in the way of architectural wonders, although it is one of the few remaining in Europe whose medieval city walls are still largely intact.

A Good Year
Russell Crowe fans will probably be aware that the Vaucluse is also the area in which *A Good Year* was filmed, a feel-good romance directed by Ridley Scott. It tells the story of a delightfully unprincipled investment banker who has forsaken the innocence of his youth for earthly pursuits (this is turning out to be a recurrent theme of this post). Ultimately, he predictably rediscovers his roots and returns to them. Cliché, cliché, cliché. Having said that, it is an enjoyable time-passer if you are at a loose end.

Some of the locations used in the film are quite stunning and most are to be found in the area which we visited. The restaurant run by Crowe's lover in the film is to be found in the Hotel Renaissance in the hill-top town of Gordes, a lovely little place largely built of thinnish slabs of hewn stone. Interestingly enough, some 10 minutes away is the town of Roussillon, although its architecture would suggest that the distance must surely be many times greater. There it is not roughly hewn stone which features prominently but rather the many shades of ochre which are to be found in the earth below and surrounding its homes and other buildings.

Small world
And here is another cliché: it is a small world. Yet, like most clichés it is true, or at least seems to be so. In an email to our friend, April, in Mullumbimby, Australia, Vicki had mentioned that we were planning to head down to the Provence to see Frédéric Pignon. It turns out that April has a sister who lives in the area and she put us in touch with her.

Zella was equally enthusiastic and suggested we meet at Pignon's show. I am very grateful that she did. Not only is she a delightful person but she also managed to arrange an impromptu meeting with

Frédéric Pignon. Thanks to a thunderstorm, that meeting turned out to be even better than envisaged.

Eqi Cheval Libre

So off we went to Pignon and Delgado's new show. Staged on the banks of what appeared to be a large man-made lake west of Monteux, Eqi Cheval Libre turned out to be an eclectic mix of liberty work, classical dressage, vaulting and stunt riding choreographed to create a diversity of moods featuring thematic combinations of music, song, props and lighting.

More than anything else, I was keen to see Frédéric Pignon's liberty work and I was not disappointed. I could wax lyrical about the interaction between him and his stallions and geldings. Instead, I have posted a number of videos which feature them in action during the show. What I especially value is the fact that the horses are not trained to heed cues like robots but are free to express themselves. Sometimes they take off in moves that are clearly not choreographed and yet they return to continue with something else. Very special! Of course, no video can replace the real thing, so if you have the chance, do not miss it. Yes, you may find something to criticise but you will also find magic to inspire you.

Frédéric Pignon

During the last part of the show I noticed an advancing thunderstorm behind the stage. Lightning was visible in the distance, accompanied by a remote rumbling. Yet we were spared until some 10 minutes after the show had ended. We were waiting to meet Frédéric Pignon as arranged on the spot by Zella (this lady is on the ball), when all of a sudden sheets of rain driven by a howling wind drove us into a tent which served as a shop. There signing books for happy visitors was the man himself chatting away in French but looking slightly dazed.

Vicki and I were introduced to Frédéric Pignon and we spent valuable time on small talk, as one does. I had the feeling that the man was physically present but mentally absent. He had been active with horses and humans for more than two hours and was now searching for things to talk about with perfect strangers as part of the public relations exercise which invariably accompanies such events. A few minutes later we thanked him for his time and left him to continue with the next lot of demanding individuals.

The thunderstorm, however, refused to allow any of us to leave the tent without a drenching, so we all bided our time. It was then that I spotted Pignon standing near the entrance, waiting for a break in the downpour to make his exit, and he was on his own. I did not hesitate. My opening question clearly took him be surprise. "Frédéric," I asked, "what do you think is the most important thing you need in order to be able to do what you do with horses." He looked at me as though I had presented him with a watermelon. This was clearly not going to be small talk.

And then he recovered and I could sense him move firmly and confidently into familiar territory. "You need to be able to work with what the horses give you." My quote may be out by a word or two as I am reporting from memory but essentially this was what he said.

Of course, I did not let it go there. The thunderstorm was clearly working in my favour. I told him that I had seen his brother, Jean-Francois, work with his horses in the Netherlands a few years before (see my post entitled *Turning on the Light – Part I* in *In Search of the Master Dancing with Horses: Challenge*) and that I noticed a pronounced difference between what he did and what Frédéric does with horses. Frédéric put it down to the fact that his brother works with mares, while he prefers to interact with stallions and geldings.

As Frédéric Pignon put it, you can be a bit more assertive with mares and perhaps to a slightly lesser extent with geldings. Stallions, however, are far more demanding. According to Frédéric, you do not ask stallions to do anything. Instead, you suggest what they may want to do and you work with what you get.

I asked Frédéric Pignon whether he knew of Klaus Ferdinand Hempfling. He said that he did. I mentioned that Hempfling maintains that the human always needs to be fully present with a horse and that anything less than 100% is not enough. Frédéric

Pignon agreed completely, noting that this is especially true for stallions. And then the rain eased.

No ego

There are prominent horse people who have learned from their horses and there are those that have to some extent. Those who have fully learned the lesson of the horse have as much ego as their equine friends: none, or at least none that is offensively in your face.

Our first observation of Frédéric Pignon in the flesh was at the outdoor café-restaurant next to the Lac du Monteux shortly before the show was due to start. He was part of a group sitting at a long table next to ours. It was a plastic-chair affair, basic without pretensions. I must confess that it was a heady relief from the enveloping presence of those deriding the evil of narcissism in our modern age while exercising every effort to ensure a general awareness that perfection is equivalent to their presence on this lovely earth.

A month in the Provence

Frédéric Pignon is hoping to organise a liberty dressage clinic in the Provence in September. Alternatively, the show may be touring Belgium. It is all a bit in the air.

Whatever the case, Zella has invited Vicki and myself to look after her home and dog while she is overseas later this year. We have agreed to do so and are now investigating the possibility of taking our horses with us and possibly, just quite possibly, arranging to have lessons with Frédéric Pignon. I will keep you posted.

Healing the Horse

15 September 2014

Here in the Netherlands we are currently blessed with a warm, sunny start to the autumn. As the trees begin to burn bronze at the edge and the first leaves parachute to the ground, the acorns and chestnuts are dropping while the season's mushrooms and toadstools are springing up in their shade in time for us to admire them. Kept from the forest by swarms of horse flies throughout the summer, Pip, Anaïs, Vicki and myself have ventured back in to reclaim our right to share its sheltered groves and scented paths. After months of trudging on tarmac roads between fields of maize and other crops, the mares are nice and forward, relishing their return to the relatively wild conditions of the woods. And as they walk beside us, I turn to my horse, scan her moving body and marvel at her healing.

Balanced horse

Pip is now overtracking nicely on both sides as she learns to carry herself in balance. The body balancing or straightness training, as some are wont to call it, is really helping her no end, as is the focused trimming of her feet. I lift her right forehoof and am stunned by how it has changed. We now have concavity in it and the sole is thicker and healthier than it has ever been. Yes, it has taken a long time as we are now two years and four months down the track. But what a change.

In her body too I see the fruits of our endeavours, as well as those of Equine Touch. A few months ago Pip's lumbar region was still quite stiff and I could not get my fingers under her scapula to vibrate the subscapularis muscle on either side. Now I am beginning to see her sacrum area swing a little more loosely and can perform the subscapular move on both sides.

When we started out, Pip was stronger on the left than on the right. This has now switched, as her body seeks to readjust to moving in a balanced fashion. Although the pain and stiffness have largely left her shoulders, she is now finding it a bit difficult to flex fully to the left, even though she steps under quite beautifully on this side. It is a very temporary affair, I feel, as we head into the cooler months.

ET practitioner diploma

Speaking of Equine Touch, after a three-month wait Vicki and I have finally received our practitioner diploma. The culmination of far more work than we had originally envisaged, this Equine Touch practitioner diploma is official recognition that we have mastered the theory and practice of this marvellous equine bodywork diploma to the extent that we are now capable of offering our services as professional Equine Touch practitioners.

I am particularly chuffed, because both of us managed to complete our studies with a final mark in excess of 90%. In addition, our practical work examiner, Lyn Palmer, who is the most experienced Equine Touch practitioner and instructor, felt that we were the most accomplished bodyworkers in practical terms who had completed the final practical assessment.

Ultimately though, the horse is the most objective assessor of our Equine Touch skills and my Pip is anything but easy to please when it comes to bodywork. Extremely sensitive, as most chestnut mares seem to have a reputation for being, Pip has required that I adopt an exceedingly resourceful approach to our Equine Touch sessions. But they are paying off, if the improved condition of her body is anything to go by.

Wauters and body awareness

Our series of five lessons with Jason Alexander Wauters has come to an end and I find myself weighing up the gains for Pip and myself. As the former star student of Klaus Ferdinand Hempfling's only full-time one year schooling programme, it is clear to me that Jason owes much of his proficiency (and perhaps a few little quirks) to the master who dances with horses. Yet Jason has managed to redefine what he has learned to present it as part of his unique blend of power, sensitivity, grace and joy.

For myself, I truly valued the opportunity to experience some of Hempfling's body awareness exercises again, albeit repackaged and represented in Jason's inimical way. It has also been a highly beneficial experience to have an instructor explain the theory of liberty work and help with its implementation in practice, while avoiding a mechanical approach. An awareness of the horse as a fellow energetic being that is also highly responsive to variations in the nuances of energy presence is essential to this approach.

Pip's past

Pip, I sense, has benefitted as much if not more from Jason's lessons. During the first lesson it was immediately clear to Jason that Pip was a victim of her past. At liberty she was prone to anxiety and panic in the absence of any other horses and when anything was demanded of her she had learned to protect herself by doing what was asked of her while isolating herself from any contact with the human making demands of her.

Jason's lessons with Pip and myself were designed to help us establish contact at liberty and to raise Pip's energy levels to the degree required for liberty work without her feeling threatened and while maintaining a connection between us. Ultimately, we were seeking to open the lines of communication between horse and human and develop the trust required to do that at a heightened level of activity.

Because of Pip's propensity to anxiety and panic at liberty, especially in a large open space, the use of a 12-metre square picadero was quite helpful, as it seemed to give her some form of reassurance. Initially, my mare just stood in the corner and shut herself off from everything, even when I entered the picadero and stood a few metres away from her.

Opening communication

Under Jason's guidance we sought to change this by raising the energy beyond the level where the horse would be desensitised to the stimulus but by doing so in a non-threatening manner. At the start I was directed to move straight from one side of the picadero to the other while gently waving a whip with a small piece of plastic attached to the drop lash in the air but far enough away from Pip so as not to constitute a threat yet not so far as to be easily ignored, while ignoring her to the extent that all I was aware of was the presence of her energy. What Pip did was her responsibility. She kept an eye on this crazy man walking from one side of the picadero to the other and simply moved away, if she felt I was too close, employing more energy the closer I was to her. Within one or two practice sessions after the lesson, Pip immediately acknowledged me when I entered the picadero and stood still.

Once Pip was used to this routine and did not feel threatened by it, in a subsequent lesson I now adopted a more direct approach. Essentially I would be doing the same thing but this time I moved directly to where she was standing and occupied that space without paying her any direct attention. Because my movement was directed towards the spot where she was standing, it had the effect of boosting her energy levels, with the result that she moved more quickly. Yet, because my energy was not directed against her but simply towards occupying the spot, her initial alarm soon faded. She was now beginning to find this interesting rather than threatening, even though her energy levels were raised. Within a few practice sessions after learning this routine, Pip not only acknowledged my presence when I entered the picadero, she also turned towards me.

Lungeing at liberty

The next step was to start establishing direct contact with Pip. First I would raise both her and my energy levels by occupying her space but this time when she moved off I was to turn to her and ask her to move forward but then immediately step back and invite her to come to me after she had taken a few steps. This was the most difficult

190

part of the training. Partly as expected, Pip immediately felt threatened the moment I started to ask her to move forward. She would flex her head and neck backwards towards me to ascertain the nature of the threat but she readily came when I invited her to follow me as I stepped backwards. Yes, her fear was evident but we now had a connection, whereas in the past we did not, and it was possible to banish fear within a few steps by inviting her to come to me, rewarding her with praise and a treat.

Some of our practice sessions after this went very pear-shaped and I was almost ready to stop. Vicki suggested that it might help if I were to lower my own energy level. Ready to try anything, I did and Pip responded accordingly. She was far less apprehensive and we had a connection which allowed me to ask her to move around the picadero at walk while raising and lowering the pace without her feeling threatened. She would then come to me when I stepped back and invited her to do so. Once she was with me I rewarded her.

Trust and energy

A number of things became very clear to me during these lessons. The most relevant was just how important it is to achieve the appropriate level and quality of the energy that is required to establish communication and trust with a horse. The human needs to be fully focused and in the moment, if they are to be sensitive enough to produce a type of energy which is light and playful, like that of a child, the type which breaks down communication barriers and instils trust, paradoxically with the aid of the indirect but dominant approaches outlined above. The pure mechanics of employing lungeing theory at liberty is simply not enough, not unless all you are trying to do is to drive a horse around in a circle, the very thing that drove Pip to learn how to move on autopilot in order to protect herself in the past.

It is rather interesting to see how this breakthrough is now reflected in my other activities with Pip. Our body balancing (a.k.a. straightness training) sessions are a case in point. Pip is now much more focused on me than she was in the past. This is making it much easier for us to do shoulder-in at the trot on a loose lead. The liberty sessions enable Pip to learn how to carry herself, something which is absolutely essential, if she is ever to carry me as well.

Riding

This brings me to riding. With all the healing that my horse is experiencing, I am now toying with the idea of making the first direct step towards riding later this month or sometime in October.

It is not only Pip who needs to prepare herself for this. So too do I. Vicki has suggested that 75 kg is a good target weight, if I wish to ride without overburdening my mare. When I last weighed myself a few weeks ago, I was on 82.5 kg. This means that I have some shedding to do. Even then, I would not seriously consider asking Pip to carry my target weight for any lengthy period of time. I am very conscious of the fact that a horse's back was not designed to carry a human. If Pip shows me – and a horse is quite capable of revealing this to anyone who cares to know – that carrying a human, in this case me, is too much for her, I am committed to getting off her and never getting on again. This is the very least I can do for my horse.

Hempfling's Iceberg and Pip's Sea
27 October 2014

Some time after I started the series, Towards Riding (see my post entitled *Towards Riding 1: The Horse* and raised the question of To Ride or Not to Ride (see my post entitled *Towards Riding 2 – To Ride or Not to Ride?*), Vicki drew my attention to the fact that some of my posts were being quoted in Chuck Mintzlaff's Friendship Training group on Facebook. Since then the question of whether to ride or not has also been raised in other Facebook groups, including one devoted to a study of Klaus Ferdinand Hempfling's ideas. Given the influence which Hempfling has had on my own thoughts concerning horses and his approach towards horse-human interaction, I thought it might be helpful to reconsider his views on the question of whether to ride or not, if for no other reason than that it differs so fundamentally from anyone else's. Then, after I started writing this post, Pip chipped in and added her input. And then shortly after that I received a copy of a book scheduled for publication with a request for feedback and it contained confirmation of Pip's input.

To ride or not to ride?
So how does Hempfling answer this question? Does he weigh up the moral issues involved? Does he consider the effects of riding on a horse's health? Does he actually consider the question at all?

The short and simple answer is this. To ride or not to ride? is a question that simply has no place in Hempfling's writings. He simply does not consider it. Neither does he bother with any of the moral, health or other dilemmas that the question may pose. Or at least he does not do so directly.

The iceberg of riding

In his book, The Horse Seeks Me, Hempfling devotes an entire page to a graphic depiction of riding as part of his overall approach to horse-human interaction. It takes the form of a tall triangle whose base is at the bottom of the page (p. 315). Of the entire triangle riding represents no more than a tiny tip at its apex. Hempfling refers to the triangle as the "iceberg of riding" and notes that "riding is its smallest part".

Indeed, the message is driven home by the situation of the chapter on riding and its length in relation to that of the book as a whole. Of all of the 343 pages that make up the book, only 41 deal with riding. That is a mere 12%. As such, riding rests on a huge base of preparation representing 88% of the book and probably an even smaller part of the tip of the iceberg of riding depicted in it. And where is it situated? Right at the end of the book.

Here is some food for thought: ask yourself what percentage riding represents of the time that you spend interacting with your horse. Where you go with the answer is up to you.

The rest of the iceberg

So what is the rest of the iceberg? Immediately below riding we find the segments of the triangle which deal with training and all of it takes place on the ground. First there is "Lungeing" and "The Dance, which are preceded by "Correction in Detail" and "Leading". The latter is an important first step to any training within Hempfling's paradigm. In other words, only the top end of Hempfling's iceberg below riding concerns training, significantly less than half, and all of it comprises groundwork.

Before training we find the segments that deal with the establishment of a connection between horse and human, without which all training and riding are impossible. Working from the bottom up, this entails "Recognising" (or characterising) the horse, followed by the "First Encounter", which consists of "Closeness and Distance", "Trust and Dominance", and "Healing". If this goes as it should, the result should be the "First Parallel", where horse and human intuitively move in synchronicity with each other. The connection has been established.

All of this rests on a base which Hempfling calls "Personal Development" and which is divided into two layers. The upper one is "Body Awareness" and the lower one, upon which the entire iceberg rests, is "Spiritual Awareness". Within Hempfling's approach towards the horse-human relationship nothing meaningful is possible with horses without this personal development.

Personal development and the horse
Now just consider the breakdown of Hempfling's iceberg for a moment. I will not even attempt to describe what each collection of segments entails, because I would need a book (or more) to do so. Suffice it to say that many aspects of them are covered in this blog.

Although personal development (body and spiritual awareness) may occur simultaneously with interaction between horse and human, it is obvious that you would require a certain level of development before you could achieve a true connection with a horse. It is also clear that you would need a more advanced level of development, if you wanted to start training a horse. Indeed, the more advanced the training that you seek to pursue, the higher the level of development that you would require.

When to ride?
So at what stage does Hempfling advise you to consider riding a horse, if you are intent on doing so? Do you first have to complete a comprehensive course of dressage or any other form of horse training on the ground before you get on? Hempfling is utterly dismissive of this approach. He writes, "As I see it, dressage training is therefore the attempt to make a functioning device out of a natural being" (p. 318). Indeed, implicit in his approach is that the same is true of any form of horse training which seeks to install technical mechanisms of control in a living being.

What is required is the development of your spiritual and bodily prowess to enable you to develop a close relationship with your horse and to be able to use your body to move as one with your equine friend. In Hempfling's words:

> all of the questions of insecurity, becoming acquainted, trust and understanding when interacting with a horse must come before you first get on the horse – before riding – because only then can they be really treated and answered. Being on the horse is just harvesting the fruits. On the horse, you can no longer thoroughly heal and no longer thoroughly correct.

(p. 320)

In fact, Hempfling is emphatic that, as long as there are problems on the ground, there will be problems in the saddle:

Problems on the ground and misunderstandings are either transferred quite clearly and visibly to riding or are hidden in one way or another. But they are always there! I have never met a horse-human pair that was an exception to this. (p. 316)

Those of us who have witnessed world champion dressage riders experiencing difficulties while leading their horses might wish to bear this in mind when next we see them achieve another ridiculously high score in an international competition.

It is also worth noting that, when explaining his approach to riding in both The Horse Seeks Me and his videos, Hempfling resurrects the horse with whom he enjoyed the closest relationship, the sensitive chestnut gelding, Janosch. This is the only horse that we ever get to see Hempfling riding without any tack at all. We may also wish to bear in mind that those and all of the other images featuring Hempfling astride a horse which are publicly available date from well before the end of the last century with only one exception, Habanero, the small, black stallion belonging to his then body awareness coach, Jo Ross, whom he trained and rode during the one-year course which Vicki and I were supposed to attend. It is clear that to Hempfling riding is a special activity which only becomes relevant after the lengthy preparation of both horse and human but predominantly the latter.

The implications

Not much imagination is required to conclude that the implications of Hempfling's approach are potentially profound. In the first place, some if not most of us will never achieve what is required on the ground before contemplating riding. Within Hempfling's approach riding is the prerogative of the few who manage to achieve the spiritual and bodily level of personal development required to befriend and guide a horse without force or restraint. And the few who manage to achieve such a level of personal development will only be ready to ride after lengthy preparation.

Viewed from Hempfling's perspective, it is clear that the vast majority of people who currently relate to their horses with their bums should not be riding or at least not yet and their horses would be far better off if they were to dismount now and stay off them until they (the horse and they human) are ready, if ever. It is also clear that as part of the Hempfling approach those few horses that would be ridden without force or restraint would also be far better off.

To those horse riders who maintain that they use a "bit of Hempfling" in their approach towards horses, training and riding, it should be starkly clear that you have profoundly misunderstood what Hempfling is about. You may be using "bits" but you are definitely not "doing Hempfling", for the chances are that, if you really were, you would not be riding or at least not yet.

Destiny

You may be aware that I have spent much of this year preparing Pip and myself for riding. Originally, I had hoped to ride my mare in the spring but postponed it, because I felt that we still needed to address her insecurity at liberty. October was to be the month in which it was finally going to happen, until destiny intervened.

In the second week of October I pulled the calf muscle in my right leg, while Vicki and I were running with the horses in the forest. Rest was required and I acceded, if only in relative terms. Just as I seemed to be recovering disaster struck. Pip came down with an injury which caused her to go lame in her right foreleg. Last week the vet conducted a sonar scan and confirmed that she has injured her deep digital flexor tendon at the level of the distal check or accessory ligament. Fortunately, it is a general swelling rather than a tear with no sign of any external force but it is serious enough to put Pip out of all but tightly controlled physical action for at least six months.

For the moment Pip is confined to a small enclosure with a walk-in, walk-out stable, which opens onto a small adjoining field, where she grazes during the day. Her enclosure is next to that of the herd, so she is still able to maintain contact with the other horses and Anaïs in particular. Every day I walk her for five minutes, hose her leg down with cold water and then apply some gel with an unpronounceable name, which the vet insists on. In addition, Pip is also on homeopathics for a few days. So far the swelling remains unchanged. Vicki and I bring the mares together at times to interact with each other and us while we try out various liberty exercises (in Pip's case, those that do not involve anything more than the movement of a body part).

Pip's input
Although I cannot explain how this accident happened, it comes as no surprise to me that it has affected Pip's vulnerable leg. With its long toe and underrun heels coupled with constant movement on the hard surface of the enclosure in which our horses are kept, the tendons in that leg were always going to be a bit vulnerable, although the progress which Pip has made over the past couple of years and which are documented in this blog led me to believe that such an injury would be unlikely.

What I did not take into account was the distinct possibility of an injury due to herd dynamics within a relatively confined space. At roughly the same time that Pip came down with her injury, we discovered a rather large hoofprint on Anaïs' hindquarters just to the right of her tail with some hair missing from the place where the toe must have made impact. I suspect that the mares were standing together, when Anaïs got kicked and both of them took evasive action with Pip twisting her vulnerable leg in the process. The absence of any evidence of external force would seem to confirm such or a similar scenario.

Pip's input as I now see it is that riding her is no longer an option that I am willing to consider, even once she has recovered. The chances of a recurrence are simply too great. Pip is never going to be ridden again. End of story. This is the least I can do for my equine friend. Perhaps I was mad to ever consider the possibility, especially with her history. What was I thinking?

The power of words

A couple of days after the vet's visit I received the draft of a book from a young woman whom I met at the Nevzorov Haute Ecole clinic hosted by Michael Bevilacqua and Cloé Lacroix in Québec, Canada, in 2012. It documents her journey and that with her horses, telling a story and containing insights which resonate deeply within me partly because of similarities of experience and partly because of what Pip seems to be showing me now.

One of the questions this book raises in relation to my interaction with Pip or any other horse concerns the extent to which I am prepared to go, the things I am willing to do and the tools I choose to resort to in order to ride. To be specific, this powerful book poses the question as to whether I would go to that extent, do those things and use those tools on and with a creature whom I claim to love and call a friend. This is a highly confronting question and, if I am to look at myself in the mirror and be very honest with the person I see in it, and I simply have to say that I can no longer do it. If love is liberating, then I want Pip to be as free as the sea within the confines of its shores.

So what now?

Now a whole new experience has begun. Pip and I are going to have to learn to find new ways of interacting with each other. I have never been down this path before, so it will be an entirely new experience. Already I can see some benefits. Pip is having to spare her vulnerable leg and rely more on her relatively underdeveloped left foreleg. This should help her greatly. We will be learning new games to keep her muscles strong while she is relatively inactive. There will no longer be any possibility of the prospect of riding bringing any pressure to bear on our relationship. In addition, because Vicki and I now need to exercise the mares separately from each other, we are weaning them off their virtual dependence on each other's company.

At this point in time I do not know whether Pip will ever return to the herd at her current livery yard. I rather suspect that it is quite possible she will not. Although the principle of keeping horses in a herd is fairly sound, the facilities need to be adequate for the number of horses involved. To a large extent they are with one major exception. There are only two entrances to the large indoor area to which the horses have free access. One is large enough to accommodate several horses at the same time, while the other can only accommodate one. All too often I have seen a commotion in the indoor area, with the result that up to ten or more horses simultaneously rush towards the exits but not all of them can fit through at the same time. The twisting and turning that then ensues has long seemed to me to be an accident waiting to happen. At this point in time I am not sure that I am prepared to put Pip back into such a situation again.

Where that will take us, is a question for the future. For the moment Pip is out of the herd and on the mend. That is enough for now.

In the moment

in the moment
now
feel the air
   flow soft and cool
hear the croon
   of doves calling
see the clouds
   smudge the water
smell the earth
   rich with promise
taste the salt
   of grateful tears

at one with
the glowing motion
of the present
grounded to the earth

yesterday's pain
tomorrow's fear
have no place
in the moment
that is always
now

Epilogue

Although this is an ongoing story, it seems fitting to end this book here. It is just so appropriate that this chapter of my journey comes to a close with a commitment to releasing my horse and her human from the impending pressure of my bum on her back and all of the connotations that unfortunate relationship of body parts has had across the species for far too long. True, my disappointment is deep but not nearly so profound as my concern for the health of my equine friend.

It is painful for Pip that destiny has had to sacrifice her limb, if only temporarily, to shout a message at me that has perhaps been looming off-stage for some time. If I am to be disarmingly honest, I must confess that Pip and I had not reached the stage where it would have been possible for me to ride her in natural collection, although I secretly hoped that we would discover that magic together once I was astride her. Riding her in the absence of self-carriage would have inevitably inflicted discomfort, if not pain on her. How do I know? Quite simply, it is the message that many horses have given me through my fingers as I have performed Equine Touch on their worn bodies. And if discomfort and pain are the price Pip would have to pay to gratify my pleasure in riding her in the absence of self-collection, there is a question that I simply cannot avoid asking. Would I really want to inflict that on a friend, one whom I publicly proclaim to love?

Perhaps there is more. Maybe I have simply not yet acquired the level of personal development which Hempfling insists is a prerequisite for anyone to indulge in what he considers to be a "highly spiritual as well as highly physical activity": riding a horse (*The Horse Seeks Me*, p. 310). For if I had, would I not have refused to allow my horse to live in conditions in which her health could be greatly compromised, as is now revealed to be the case? Would I not have had the wisdom to take her elsewhere when the number of horses in the herd exceeded what was safe in the situation in which they are required to live? Would I not have acquired the ability to discern what would be safe for her and what not? Have I not let my friend, Pip, down because my personal development has been lacking?

Maybe I have but perhaps I have not. Yet one thing is certain, such recrimination is a form of self-indulgence which has no place in my relationship with my mare. It can serve neither of us any good and, worse, it draws attention away from where it is required now: how to help Pip both to heal and to find a new way of living fully in the absence of much movement while relatively cut off from her herd, an alien condition for any horse. The question that really drives me at present is how I can be the kind of human she would still choose to be with in these difficult circumstances.

Essentially, it is no different from the very question that launched me into the search for a new way of being with horses and ultimately of just being, a search which ultimately drove me to leave Australia with my wife, a horse and a dog bound for Denmark and the man who claimed that he could show me just how to answer that question, a journey that would ultimately result in the Horses and Humans blog and now this book and its prequel: *In Search of the Master Who Dances with Horses*. When I left Australia the master who dances with horses had an identity – a face and a name – and a rather well-known one at that. Since then he has earned a level of fame on social media which not even widely known horse trainers such as Monty Roberts and Pat Parelli can rival. Klaus Ferdinand Hempfling was the master who dances with horses, to me anyway. And I was but one of a growing number of people who felt the same way.

In the course of my journey, much of which is documented in these pages, I have learned many lessons. The most important of these I have endeavoured to set out in my posts on the blog and now in these books. Yet perhaps the most important lesson that I have learned is this. The true master who dances with horses is someone whom horses not only look to for care and guidance but perhaps more importantly for the opportunity of dancing through life together. Yet why would a horse want to do this with another species, one that has earned a reputation for meting out unbridled cruelty not only to its own kind but also every other, and still does? The simple answer to this is that a horse does not befriend a species, only another creature who is capable sharing the joy that the dance of life has to offer. This may be another horse but in my experience, however limited it may be, it may also be a human and, as such, may also be you and I.

Ultimately, the true master who dances with horses was waiting for me to discover him not in Denmark but within me. And essentially, it was the horse – represented by those with whom I have been privileged to spend time together – that has helped me embark on the journey of discovering that master. At the end of it all, I need not have left Europe to emigrate to the other side of the world to find that master. Neither did I need to leave Australia for Denmark to find him. For he has been waiting inside for me to discover all along. And yet, I am aware that without the experiences that I have had, I would not be discovering him now in the same way that I am.

As you go on your journey through life, perhaps you are searching for a new way of being with horses. If you are, perhaps you may wish to be aware that, if pursued in all honesty while guided by an unswerving, unconditional love for your horse, you are likely to find more than you bargained for. It is my belief that there is a master who dances with horses waiting within each one of us until the day we learn to look inside and find that master instead of chasing after external illusions as I have done. It is my wish that you will find the master who dances with horses within you, for your horse will benefit enormously and so will you. And if both of you do, then we are one step closer to a better world.

Be well!
Andrew

Also available

If you have not yet read the prequel to this book, you can also find it obtain it where you found this one. It is called *In Search of the Master Who Dances with Horses: Challenge.*

An invitation...

If you have found this book worth reading and are in agreement with the approach towards horses which it advocates, may I invite you to leave a positive review on the website of the retailer where you purchased it. The more positive reviews there are, the more likely it is to be read by other humans who are looking for a more horse-friendly way of being with their horses.

Feel free to contact me

Feedback is welcome. You may email me at liamsga@gmail.com or contact me through my Facebook page at https://www.facebook.com/andrewglynsmail. Horses and Humans also has a publications page on Facebook at https://www.facebook.com/horsesandhumans and a group page at https://www.facebook.com/groups/horsesand humans/. Please feel free to join the Horses and Humans group and make a contribution to helping people become the kind of human a horse seeks to be with. The Horses and Humans blog may be found at www.horsesandhumans.com/blog/.

Bibliography and Other Resources

Various books are referred to throughout both volumes of *In Search of the Master Who Dances with Horses*. Here I would like to leave you with the references to those which I deem to be a vital part of my library. I have broken them down into two lists: *Essential* and *Recommended Resources*. All of the resources are books except where otherwise noted.

Essential Resources
Beck, Andy, *Horsonality*, ebook available from http://www.equine-behavior.com/Downloads/ppp.htm

Bevilacqua, Michael, *Beyond the Dream Horse: A Revealing Perspective on Attaining a True Relationship*, Equi-Forme, Quebec, 2010 (www.beyondthedreamhorse.ca)

– *Au-delà du Cheval de Rêve: Comment créer une relation authentique avec votre cheval*, Equi-Forme, Quebec, 2010 (www.beyondthedreamhorse.ca)

– *Freunde Fürs Leben: Ehrliche Partnerschaft Mit Deinem Pferd, Equi-Forme*, Quebec, 2010 (www.beyondthedreamhorse.ca)

Bowe, Andrew, *The Barefoot Blacksmith: Vol. 2. Maintenance Trimming*, The Barefoot Blacksmith, 2007 (www.barehoofcare.com)

Higgins, Gillian, *How Your Horse Moves: A Unique Visual Guide to Improving Performance*, David and Charles, Newton Abbot, 2011

– *Horses Inside Out: Movement from the Anatomical Perspective* (DVD), 2009, (www.horsesinsideout.com)

Kathrens, Ginger, *Cloud: The Wild Stallion of the Rockies Collection*, Australian Broadcasting Corporation, 2011,

(www.abcshop.com.au). The three documentaries on this DVD
are also available free of charge to viewers in North America
at www.pbs.org.
May, Stormy, *The Path of the Horse: Taking the First Step* (DVD),
Stormy May Productions, 2008 (now available free on
YouTube at
https://www.youtube.com/watch?v=TQUMAJCh1fA)
Tolle, Eckhart, *The Power of Now: A Guide to Spiritual
Enlightenment*, Hachette Australia, Sydney, 2004
– *Practising the Power of Now: A Guide to Spiritual
Enlightenment*, Hodder & Stoughton, London, 2011
A Tai Chi or Feldenkrais course with reference materials (video
and/or book) that you can take home with you.

Recommended Resources

Barclay, Harold, *The Role of the Horse in Man's Culture*, J.A. Allen,
London, 1980
Budras, K., Sack, W.O. and Röck, S, *Anatomy of the Horse*,
Schlütersche, Hannover, 2011
Clayton, H.M., Flood, P.F. and Rosenstein, D.S., *Clinical Anatomy
of the Horse*, Mosby Elsevier, Edinburgh, 2005
Delgado, Magali and Pignon, Frédéric with Walser, David, *Gallop to
Freedom: Training Horses with Our Six Golden Principles*,
Trafalgar Square, North Pomfret, 2009
Hempfling, Klaus Ferdinand, *Coming Together* (DVD), J.A. Allen,
London, 2005
– *Dancing with Horses: Collected Riding on a Loose Rein*
(book), Trafalgar Square, North Pomfret, 2001
– *Dancing with Horses* (DVD), J.A. Allen, London, 1999
– *De Boodschap van de Paarden*, Uitgeverij Karnak,
Amsterdam, 2002
– *Die Botschaft der Pferde*, Goldmann, 1998
– *The Horse Seeks Me*, Cadmos, London, 2010

Jwing-Ming, Yang, *Tai Chi Chuan: Classical Yang Style*, Second Edition (book), YMAA Publication Centre, Wolfeboro, 2010 (www.ymaa.com)

- Yang, *Tai Chi Chuan: Classical Yang Style*, Second Edition (DVD), YMAA Publication Centre, Wolfeboro, 2010 (www.ymaa.com)

Kohanov, Linda, *The Tao of Equus: A Woman's Journey of Healing and Transformation through the Way of the Horse*, New World Library, Novato, 2001

Kreile, Sigrid, *Im Bannkreis des Pferdeschamanen*, IKS, 2005

May, Stormy, *The Path of the Horse: From Competition to Compassion*, Our Horses Press, 2012 (www.ourhorses.org)

Nevzorov, Alexander, *Nevzorov Haute Ecole Principles* (DVD), Nevzorov Haute École, 2006, (www.hauteecole.ru)

- *The Horse Crucified and Risen*, Nevzorov Haute École, Charlestown, 2011 (www.hauteecole.ru)

- *The Horse Crucified and Risen: Parts I and II* (DVD), Nevzorov Haute École, (www.hauteecole.ru)

- *Tractate on a School Mount*, Nevzorov Haute École, Nevzorov Haute École, Charlestown, 2011 (www.hauteecole.ru)

Rashid, Mark, *Horses Never Lie: The Heart of Passive Leadership*, David & Charles, Cincinnati, 2000

Resnick, Carolyn, *Naked Liberty: Memoirs of My Childhood*, Amigo Publications, Los Olivos, 2005

- *Introduction to the Waterhole Rituals* (DVD), Stormy May Productions, 2008, (www.carolynresnick.com)

Ruddock, Jock, *The Equine Touch: From Zero to Hero in Your Horse's Eyes*, The Equine Touch Foundation, 2008 (www.theequinetouch.com)

Spilker, Imke, *Empowered Horses*, Trafalgar Square, North Pomfret, 2009

Veldman, Frans and Kooistra, Ilona, *Hoef Natuurlijk: Gezondere Hoeven en Betere Prestaties in Sport en Recreatie*, Paard Natuurlijk, Netherlands, 2007 (www.hoefnatuurlijk.nl)

- *Natuurlijk Bekappen* (DVD), Paard Natuurlijk, Netherlands, 2005 (www.paardnatuurlijk.nl)
- *Paard Natuurlijk: Gezondere Paarden en Betere Prestaties in Sport en Recreatie*, Paard Natuurlijk, Netherlands, 2010 (www.paardnatuurlijk.nl)